TEN LETTERS TO MONTAIGNE

"SELF" AND "OTHER"

GUERNICA WORLD EDITIONS 24

We are thankful to Eesti Kultuurkapital (Traducta)
for its support of the translation and publication

TEN LETTERS TO MONTAIGNE

"SELF" AND "OTHER"

JÜRI TALVET

Translated from the Estonian
by the author and H.L. Hix

GUERNICA
World
EDITIONS
TORONTO—BUFFALO—LANCASTER (U.K.)
2019

Original title: *Kümme kirja Montaigne'ile. "Ise" ja "teine."*
Tartu: Tartu **Ülikooli** Kirjastus, 2014
Copyright © 2014, by Jüri Talvet
Translation © 2019, Jüri Talvet, H.L. Hix and Guernica Editions Inc.

Michael Mirolla, editor
Cover design: Allen Jomoc Jr.
Interior layout: Jill Ronsley, suneditwrite.com
Author cover image: Birgit Püve
Guernica Editions Inc.
287 Templemead Drive, Hamilton (ON), Canada L8W 2W4
2250 Military Road, Tonawanda, N.Y. 14150-6000 U.S.A.
www.guernicaeditions.com

Distributors:
Independent Publishers Group (IPG)
600 North Pulaski Road, Chicago IL 60624
University of Toronto Press Distribution,
5201 Dufferin Street, Toronto (ON), Canada M3H 5T8
Gazelle Book Services, White Cross Mills
High Town, Lancaster LA1 4XS U.K.

First edition.
Printed in Canada.

Legal Deposit—Third Quarter
Library of Congress Catalog Card Number: 2019944675
Library and Archives Canada Cataloguing in Publication
Title: Ten letters to Montaigne : "self" and "other" / Jüri Talvet ; translated
from the Estonian
by the author and H.L. Hix.
Other titles: Kümme kirja Montaigne'ile. English
Names: Talvet, Jüri, author, translator. | Hix, H. L., translator.
Description: Series statement: Guernica world editions ; 24 | Translation of:
Kümme kirja
Montaigne'ile.
Identifiers: Canadiana (print) 20190116250 | Canadiana (ebook)
20190116471 | ISBN 9781771834704
(softcover) | ISBN 9781771834711 (EPUB) | ISBN 9781771834728 (Kindle)
Classification: LCC PH666.3.A45 A2 2019 | DDC 894/.54563—dc23

Acknowledgements

I am deeply grateful to International Writers and Translators' Center of Rhodes for its hospitality. While staying there from mid-November to mid-December 2011, I could write the main part of the present essay book.

Contents

LETTER 1

Cher Michel de Montaigne,

I write to you from Rhodes, the Greek island that, since you left this world, has had a complicated and bizarre history. For several centuries it was dominated by Turks, and Italians ruled here in the first half of the 20th century, but after WWII it became Greek again. From the window of my room at Rhodes' International Writers' Centre, I can see a fragment of the blue Mediterranean, with grayish Turkish mountains on the opposite shore. Directly in front of my window, a palm-tree, though half-withered, stands proudly erect, in defiant resistance to the winds. A group of crows tries to land on its crest, but the wind pushes them away, until finally they give up their enterprise and leave.

I write you because, especially in recent years, I have come to value you as a European thinker whose ideas often confirm my own meditations. Ideas similar to yours emerge also from the work of a number of brilliant writers of your time, which now we call the Renaissance. I have in mind Erasmus, Thomas More, and Rabelais, your predecessors, as well as the English poet and playwright William Shakespeare, who was inspired by your *Essays* shortly after you had passed away. Shakespeare's plays and poems are still staged and read all over the world at the start of the 21st century. Similarly, posterity has treasured, as I am sure you would have, the hefty book entitled *Don Quixote* (*Don Quijote*, in Spanish), by the Spanish novelist Miguel de Cervantes, who died in 1616, the same year as Shakespeare. In the work of a few other talented and philosophically-minded Spanish writers of the 17th century (Francisco de Quevedo, Tirso de Molina, Pedro Calderón de la Barca, Baltasar Gracián, some of whose work I have translated into my native Estonian), and that of a small number of Western writers since, you would recognize echoes of the same spiritual and mental notes that sounded in your own essays.

No doubt, you have been one of the greatest Western philosophers, but in the footsteps of Plutarch, your favourite ancient thinker, whose "authority" never mimicked that of the founders of mainstream Western philosophy, the work that now orients the official programs of philosophy courses at Western universities. In these programs, Plato and Aristotle are present, but not Plutarch. Similarly, in university courses these days, you are most often classified with writers, rather than with philosophers. Your essays are discussed as literature, not as philosophy.

Mainstream Western philosophy, as we know it at the start of the 21st century, has stayed in the shadows cast over the mind-world by Aristotle and then, after a long lapse, by philosophers at work not long after your own age: thus, your fellow-countryman René Descartes, who asserted the world of ideas and reason as superior to nature and the senses, and insisted that a person exists only as ideas. The same has been said by some influential French thinkers of the end of the 20th century, such as Jacques Derrida and Michel Foucault. Both are now dead. They inspired a whole generation of keen followers, the so-called postmodern(ist)s. By the second decade of the 21st century, however, we must doubt whether their ambitions of establishing an everlasting age of totally liberalized ideas, with no moral nucleus, can satisfy the spiritual needs of the younger generations, those born in the 1980s and after. The introduction of the prefix "post-" itself, in its attempt to determine a kind of superiority over preceding ages, their culture and creation, starts to look suspicious. Time continues its flow, annihilating all "posts," and revealing to the living world new beginnings, young love, and fresh hopes. The nameless and the undefined abolishes all names and definitions, including those concocted by the most astute among human minds.

Especially during the second half of the 19th century, science in Western countries made a powerful "leap." Political-economical power structures found it a much stronger ally than the church had been in the preceding centuries. Science, based on reason and intellect, started to drive away religion and traditions. It was something new, and brought about many technical innovations. Totally new phenomena emerged in social life and culture. The church had reminded people about the end of the world, but science created a powerful illusion of progress, a vision of the future as an earthly eternity, instead of a celestial life beyond the tomb for the virtuous and good, the only positive perspective the church could offer.

In these letters I will not go into detail about these innovations. Even if I wanted to explain them, I could not, because my knowledge and education would prove insufficient. Electricity itself, without which we cannot imagine our life since the start of the 20th century, remains a mystery to me, never mind the workings of computers, which since at least the turn of this century have offered the illusion that humankind could feed itself spiritually from apparently endless combinations of smaller illusions. The great phrase of José Ortega y Gasset, "man lives with technique, not from technique," seemed to lose its validity. Those inventing, managing, and selling computers claim earnestly that a completely new, self-sufficient morality has been and is being created by the computer world.

Yet it would be hasty to rush ahead with any too-definite conclusions. After a relatively steady development since the 18th century, the progress (at least in the West) in material welfare and economy, powerfully enhanced by science, has been blocked at the start of the 21st century by a point of doubt. Coinciding with the most euphoric apex of scientific and technological advances, the world is facing some of the deepest economic crises it has known in the Modern Age. Though science and technology have proven their capacity to produce anything, that is, any material object the human brain can imagine, it cannot cope with such a crisis. The present economic de-stabilization may be only an initial phase of future cataclysms. It may easily drive humankind into situations in which it still has to admit that "man does not live from technique."

By the way, Ortega y Gasset was not at all a conservative. In one photo taken in the 1920s or 1930s he can be seen proudly driving a car. I will not explain to you what a car is, technically. Suffice it to say that since the start of the 20th century it has become one symbol of human progress. By far more than trains—one of the main inventions of science and technology in the 19th century, the car represents individual progress. On a train you mingle with other people, in a kind of an ever changing collectivity. In a car, on the contrary, you drive either alone or with family or friends or a lover. The car symbolizes individual material welfare, the main driving force of an economic system known at least since the work of Karl Marx as "capitalist." Marx was a German Jew whose preaching about communism—an economic system based on collectivism instead of individualism—shook the very fundaments of the world's conscience and provoked some of its major revolutions at the start of the 20th century.

Cars or, as they are also called, automobiles, are mostly put into motion by gasoline, produced from crude oil. Thus, contrary to the term "automobile," they are not really "self-moving" machines. They depend on nourishment from nature. Though nature has provided the world with immense reserves of crude oil, often hidden in the sea depths, from where it is being extracted, at least by the start of the 21st century humanity has begun to realize that crude oil reserves are not infinite. Yesterday I took a long walk through the island's capital city, Rhodes. I saw a series of beautiful Mediterranean vistas, and an amazing achievement of the military science and technology of your age, the Renaissance: an immense defense castle system constructed by the Christian knights, who had to defend themselves against attacks by the Moslems, the Turks. Despite an economic crisis which has had some of its strongest effects here in Greece, I feel from Greek people in the streets and public places kindness and friendliness. Yet I was surprised to see that the main street leading to the writers' international house has no footpath for pedestrians. The road is only for cars. A pedestrian must humbly keep near outer walls of the houses, to avoid being run over by automobiles! Like all other streets of the old city of Rhodes (built many centuries ago), the street is crammed with cars, lavishly emitting smoke. Humankind is paying a high price for having put into movement these "automobiles." They are now damaging the health of all living nature, including humans themselves, not to a lesser degree than cigars or cigarettes. Smoking cigarettes has been recently banished in the public places of most European countries. However, nobody seems to question seriously whether the short-term comfort offered by cars can justify long-term massive destruction of the natural environment.

Going for the first time from the writers' house down the hill, I passed by a tiny kitten, run over by a car. Crows were taking an interest in its corpse. Car-windows defend the driver and allow the driver also to see out. However, in their private "moving home or castle," drivers tend to forget that these "autos" (as we call cars in Estonian) do not look out by their own glassy eyes, but can move without harm only if human eyes, fatally connected with one's soul, make them watch out, aware of the "other." The people of Rhodes like cats, that populate the streets. One late evening in the darkness I saw a cat in the path of a car. It was as if, when the car sped by, a sudden flash passed under it. It was quite frightening, but a second later I saw instead of the car a yellow cat, walking on the other side of the street, safe and sound—a lucky one!

* * *

In your essays you repeatedly reveal discontent with bookish and scholarly philosophy, torn away from the living reality around us and establishing its own private reign with its sophisticated language, understandable only for specialized and consecrated people, those sharing the "language technology" of the guild. I can inform you that in our days this scholarly-technological tendency has not at all exhausted itself, but on the contrary, it has shown a great vitality. I take it as a feature inherent in human nature. Most probably, it has to do with an instinct of self-preservation.

Material progress has proved that earthly wealth accrues to those who are in the vanguard of turning natural riches and resources into profit. In your days these were the great landowners and slave-traders. In our days they are called capitalists. Bankers who manage money and financial systems, based on trading money, have prospered in all times, yours and mine. The same applies to great industrialists. Diligence, cleverness, skill, active zeal—through such characteristics people who first grant their own material welfare have in doing so built up a vast subsystem of technology and specialized craftsmanship. Regardless of the degree of sophistication of their activity, they work with zeal and diligence to produce tangible things—something for society's immediate use, objects and services for which one must pay money.

At least since the second half of the 19th century—the age of a spectacular rise of natural and exact sciences, a vigorous tendency in the world's academia (universities, above all) has emerged, to turn philosophy and humanities into an auxiliary system of natural and exact sciences. Free independent meditation has gradually been replaced by thinking that relies on a specialized language technology, a kind of a formal language capable of producing an appearance of similarity to "hard science." Such thinking, ever in conformity with the great system of extracting profit from nature in the name of material comfort, following one daily fashion or other, is channelled into a labyrinth of words in which it gradually is deafened and turned mute. In the moral sense, the value of such thinking becomes non-existent.

For this reason I have grown extremely sceptical about the capacity of human sciences to contribute to virtue, which for you was the highest goal of all philosophy. In the history since your lifetime, I trust less in zealous scholars than in creative people, especially writers—free thinkers following the spirit of your philosophy. Free thinking means awakening the reading public to a wider awareness about the meaning of our earthly existence, discussing the validity of values established by the dominant economic-political power system, as well as making audible the voice of a human minority, opposed to the impositions of the reigning materialism and rationalism.

I admit that in my days many from the world intellectual body (writers and other creative people) have been skilfully manipulated by the political-economic power system and its mighty ally, the public media. Writing as well as culture and creativity in the broader sense are accepted as a kind of entertainment, something analogous to the novels of chivalry of your days (which you say you never liked). Literature and culture meant for various tastes and species of the mass public is produced in overabundance. At the same time media, well aware of human weaknesses, seduce the public by grotesquely exaggerating the audio-visual, creating a culture of copies and stereotypes, deprived of any originality. Thus is the imagination of the public intentionally and purposefully curbed and deafened, turned into vulgarity.

However, I am glad to say that even the apparently most vulnerable species of human cultural creation, poetry, has not at all disappeared from the present-day world. It resists as a nucleus of beauty and deep human consciousness. I know that you, Montaigne, highly respected poetry, even though you yourself did not write poems. In my opinion, also among other genres of literary creation—prose fiction, drama— the greatest achievements are those in which the poetic spirit, along with philosophy, has been present. There, philosophy rises on the wings of poetry to heights unachieved by the mechanical reasoning of professional philosophy. In the greatest literary works it has become audible to the widest possible public.

What more could philosophy hope to achieve? I think such literary creation is the culmination of human creativity, its purest essence. I cannot discuss all these masterpieces in my following letters, but to give you an idea of some of them, I will attach short supplements or annexes in which I try to resume the creative originality and image philosophy of a series of novels written after your lifetime. Some years ago one of Estonia's main daily newspapers asked me to write commentaries on a number of translated novels, reprints of which they launched. For these letters, I have adapted those commentaries.

* * *

Since the end of the 20th century the world has been considerably levelled, turned into a commercially homogeneous system dominated by monopolized capital. You can buy anywhere in the world nearly the same products. This process has been called "globalization." The main language supporting it is English, the language of some of the world's mightiest economic and political powers, the United States—a nation that did not exist yet in your lifetime—as well as the old neighbour and rival of France, Great Britain, whose middle class above all laid the basis for America, as we now generally call the world's superpower. Besides, English has become the native language of Australia and Canada and some smaller countries also populated by the British. As the heritage of British colonization, India and many other countries in Asia and Africa also use English as a language of communication.

Despite these facts, language barriers have not at all disappeared from the world. Some postmodern theoreticians have argued that nations have been constructed by groups of intellectuals, by purposeful, rationally-directed efforts and planning. I suspect this is at best a half-truth. With the exception of some super-nations, which for a considerable part of my own lifetime the Soviet Union (a Russian-dominated communist empire that endured for seven decades of years of the 20th century) was, nation-states in many parts of the world—and almost exclusively in Europe—are still rooted in the language predominantly spoken by a community.

Any language is a phenomenon of nature. It is a decisive factor determining a nation's individuality. Very little if any significant poetry has been created in artificial languages or in languages one has mastered by mere learning. Petrarch wrote his essays and also some of his longer poems in Latin, because it had been established, since the fall of the Western Roman Empire, as the language shared by all learned European men in the Middle Ages. However, the most appreciated part of Petrarch's work is gathered in his *Canzoniere*, a collection of lyrical poetry which the poet, despite living for long periods in France, wrote in his native Italian.

In the present-day globalization process, commercial universality has been realized by rational planning and profit-calculation. To seduce large communities to accept these products, the promotion mechanism astutely manipulates people's feelings. Thus, Americans and British pop-musicians and singers, acclaimed by the widest possible world public of young people, have substantially contributed to the triumphs of commercial globalization.

I would not object, but unfortunately all processes, material as well cultural, work in the closest inter-relation. Mass culture promotes commerce, while commerce in its turn promotes only the type of culture that serves best its business. From a thoroughly strategic-rational, commercial point of view, all world nations should abandon their native languages, and with them poetry, whose highest flights occur in its creator's mother tongue.

Yet as you have eloquently shown in your essays, untempered rationality, like any too gross materialism, sooner or later runs into trouble. I think in our time defending linguistic plurality is a way of defending nature, vitally dependent on the plurality of its species.

In composing these letter-essays in English, am not I myself, you might counter, a victim of commercial globalization? I do not think so. I have created the largest part of my work in my native Estonian. As for the larger essays and scholarly articles I have written first directly in English or Spanish, I have later adapted them into my mother tongue. And I have created all of my poetry in Estonian.

My arguments may seem strange enough to you, because in your lifetime such tiny nations as Estonia, with its population of slightly more than a million people, were not considered nations at all. At least till the end of the 18th century, their writers were forced to learn the languages of the "leading" nations, because their own languages were considered too poor, insufficient for expressing abstract or meta-physical ideas.

The powerful liberation movement in Romanticism from the end of the 18th century, however, has revealed the inadequacy of such views. After a number of revolutions and wars of liberation, even quite small European nations have achieved political independence. In the present day we take it as natural that we write in our mother language and speak it in all spheres of our nation's social life. As I have worked with several languages, I can assure you that the present day Estonian language is as rich and flexible in its forms as English or Spanish or any other language of the "leading" nations. Our writers have con-tributed to its gradual development since the national "awakening" period in the second half of the 19th century, and the contribution by translators and linguists has been enormous as well.

Naturally, certain barriers remain, especially for writers from small nations. As their reading public is utterly limited, a writer cre-ating in his/her mother language may find his/her books met with indifference, unless those books follow fashionable trends established in the Western "centres," such as France or the U.S. Under the influ-ence of public media, vulgarity becomes a general feature, a "norm," and those with taste still for good literature are silenced and driven away from the literary or cultural scene.

In such conditions it is but natural that any writer working in a minority language must make a double or triple effort to be heard outside his/her native language area. My poetry and essays have ap-peared in recent years in translated books in English, Spanish, and some other languages. But it has meant a special effort and toil for me. I myself have had to prepare "base" or literal translations, while some of my friends, writers or literarily educated people in the English or Spanish language area have adapted them into flexible literary pat-terns in their native language.

So few people outside Estonia know our language that the happy coincidence of language knowledge and poetic-mindedness is an ex-tremely rare phenomenon. I believe the best results can be achieved by a creative collaboration of a poet knowing several foreign languages and a translator/poet working on the basis of the target language or an intermediary language. The results can sometimes be surprisingly good. Thus, a short time ago some prestigious U.S. poetry journals published some translations of poems by the Estonian Juhan Liiv (1864–1913), whose work, until recently, had been in Estonia generally considered untranslatable. In this case I worked together with my friend Harvey L. Hix, an American poet who does not know Estonian well enough to translate directly from it. As English was my specialization at university, I was capable of providing "base" translations that were as exact as possible. Even so, without the help of a major Estonian-English dictionary—a genuine masterpiece by Paul F. Saagpakk, an Estonian who found refuge in America after WWII, I could hardly have hoped to prepare my initial translations in a form that would enable Harvey to cast them successfully into a definite shape.

There is one more aspect in the intercultural transmission of literary texts. My writing in English is definitely poorer than that of writers for whom English is native. However, I suppose that when I write directly in English, my language has a somewhat greater syntactic flexibility, than when it is translated from Estonian into English. Syntactic patterns differ considerably from one language to other. Even when translating my own English texts into Estonian, I feel that my Estonian syntax does not have the same flexibility as when writing a text directly in my mother language. When I can choose in which direction to translate, I definitely prefer to translate into my native language, instead of translating into a foreign language.

I am sceptical about translations made by people for whom the target language of a translation is not their native tongue. As an Estonian by birth, even with my relatively good English, learned at university, I can go only halfway. Someone who *feels* the target language from inside has to come to help me, to meet my language. Yes, it is English, but not yet the English of the natural "self." Translation is based not only on knowing the language, but even more importantly, on feeling it. Only if the language is *felt* can the core of the work from other culture be put into a dialogue with the receiving culture, its "self." Translators of literary works, especially of poetry, are "trans-knowers," but to an even greater extent, they could be called "trans-feelers" or "trans-sensors."

In writing my letters to you, a Frenchman, I should write in French, but my foreign language skills do not extend beyond writing in English, Spanish, and Russian. I have not learned to speak other Romance languages besides Spanish. Still, at least with the help of dictionaries, I can read and understand written texts. I have read your essays basically in English translation. Since its first publication in 1987, *The Complete Essays* in the English translation by M.A. Screech have been reprinted several times. It is the most complete contemporary edition of your essays in English. It has merited high praise not only by scholars but by such well-known writers as Gore Vidal. Screech's commentaries and his large introductory text provide a convincing proof that his translation is fully reliable. As the American historical fiction writer Gore Vidal has said in *The Times Literary Supplement*: "Anglophones of the next century will be deeply in Dr. Screech's debt." I may add that not only anglophones are in his debt. I am, too, as are, I imagine, many others in the world whose native tongue is not English.

LETTER 2

IT IS STRANGE. I PLANNED to write these letters in English, but somehow unconsciously I wrote today my first phrases of this second letter in Estonian.

Teie mõtteküpsuse südamikku jõudsin ma aeglaselt. Teadsin küll hästi võtmesõnu, mille abil teie vaateid on iseloomustatud.

In English it means: "I was slow to reach the core of your mature thought, though I knew well the key terms by which your views had been characterized."

Estonian is one of the Finno-Ugric languages. Only three communities relying on these languages have at the start of the 21st century their own (internationally recognized independent) states: Hungary, Finland and Estonia. A number of smaller Finno-Ugrian nationalities live within Russia, near the Urals, the borderland between Europe and Asia: Mordovians, Maris, Udmurts, and some others. Unlike the great majority of European nations, we Finno-Ugrians are not Indo-Europeans. Our language system differs considerably from those of the major Indo-European language families: Germanic, Romance, and Slavic.

Language has been increasingly important in Western philosophy. In its newest stage, the Frenchman Jacques Derrida and his followers have deduced their discourses almost exclusively from French, including playful application of homophonic words with various meanings. It is funny to observe what efforts Derrida's numerous postmodern addicts in Eastern Europe have made, to translate his works into their languages. The best-known example is Derrida's ambiguous application of the terms "différence" and "différance," both derived from the French verb "différer." It has two meanings: "to defer" and "to differ." It is quite natural that any attempt to translate this ambiguity into a language with a totally different semantic and morphologic system, would be a vain *tour de force*.

In some of his works, Derrida has tried to criticize "logo-centrism," deriving in that case "logos" from innate (spoken) language, as adapted by a community (Ferdinand de Saussure's "language"). However, paradoxically, by making written language and writing in the broadest sense the very core of his philosophy, Derrida himself has established a system of logo-centrism, which at the same time becomes identical with an extreme kind of anthropocentrism. Its basis is "I," "myself," my "own"—an intellectual speculation in "my language," French," beyond which the rest of the world becomes practically nonexistent.

Derrida's philosophy stands in radical opposition to yours. You mention the ancient philosopher Zeno, who among his disciples characterized some as "philologos" and others as "logophilos." The former studied languages, to understand thoughts and realities beyond them. The latter studied languages as something self-sufficient, containing all reality and all thoughts in themselves. In that sense, Derrida could be qualified as the postmodern "prince of logophiloi."

In my recent works, I frequently use the term "symbiosis," which shares, I think, the reconciliatory line in your essays that avoids extremes. In this case, both the spoken and the written language are important. Language mediates between realities, being the fundamental means of communication in any sphere of existence. It is not self-sufficient, but is constantly attacked and modified by changing realities of which it is part. Realities, too, are deeply influenced by language.

Those who dominate speech, the great preachers and orators, have had traditionally a magic spell on vast human communities. Orators' skills have always been a major advantage in political life.

Many dictators have been highly talented orators. I do not think the communist system in Cuba, as established after their revolution in 1959, would have endured so long without the magic spell of the public speeches of their great *comandante* Fidel Castro. As his biographers have shown, Castro learned a lot from the speeches of Benito Mussolini, the Italian fascist dictator.

However, such spontaneous speaking by heart—Castro was famous for being able at his political apex to speak in front of huge crowds of people for four hours or more without pause—can hardly be learned and achieved by training or exercise. It is a talent provided by nature, something akin to all artistic creation. It may be one of the reasons why some of the dictators—the same kind of Mussolini and Castro—have also had a special spell to writers and intellectuals.

It is also true that despite all their evident sins Mussolini and Castro did not build concentration camps or commit atrocities on such a large scale as Hitler and Stalin, the worst monster-dictators of the first half of the 20th century. Thus the American poet Ezra Pound, who created his work under the influence of oriental philosophy and poetics, was a great admirer of Mussolini, while one of the most significant novel writers of the second half of the 20th century, the Colombian Gabriel García Márquez, remained a faithful friend of Fidel Castro.

Notwithstanding the spell of these orators-dictators, it is quite clear that in reality they were wrong in their ideas. By the magic of their language they have caused their people and societies a lot of suffering. Thus language itself, oral or written, even though mastered to perfection in some of its aspects, does not automatically grant great depth of wisdom.

This indicates that meditating about language(s), their coincidences and differences, in an attempt to understand realities (and ideas, as a part of reality), is necessary and productive, especially if we avoid extreme positions. Thus I am far from asserting that my language, Estonian, is perfect at its present stage. I do not wish to oppose it to languages with larger cultural traditions and idealize it as something "savage," "primeval," and, as such, capable of sustaining a kind of philosophy close to the origins of humankind (which anyway seems to have started its contradictory development in the forest, or *silva* in Latin). I only suggest that including examples from languages belonging to different families could provide philosophically-inclined discourses a means to avoid becoming monologues. It could enhance a dialogue between "own" and "other," that is, the understanding of realities through differences, which yet do not exclude elements of intersection.

Thus if you look at my phrase in Estonian and English, at the start of the present letter, you will notice that while in English "I" (in Estonian: *mina* or *ma*) is positioned at the beginning of the phrase, in Estonian it is located in the latter part of the sentence or is omitted altogether. In our technologized age, computers can provide mechanically-made translations between different languages. Because it is incapable of mastering the flexibility of a natural language, the computer would translate my phrases word by word:

"The core of your mature thought reached I slowly."

English and especially German are reluctant to admit flexible word order, which is a very common feature in Estonian. In that sense our language is closer, for instance, to Spanish (a language that, like Italian, you knew very well): *Al núcleo de su pensamiento maduro llegué despacio.* There is another coincidence with Spanish in that Estonian can easily omit personal pronouns in front of verbs. Thus, I could have said: *Teie mõtteküpsuse südamikku jõudsin aeglaselt*, thus omitting *ma* (I). I could likewise have written: *Ma jõudsin aeglaselt teie mõtteküpsuse südamikku*, or *Jõudsin aeglaselt teie mõtteküpsuse südamikku*. Had I used the larger (complete) form of "I," *mina*, instead of the abbreviated form *ma*, I would have given to my phrase a shade of artificiality admissible in special literary style. Also by doing so, I would have stressed particularly my own person, "I."

Not having "I" in the initial position of a phrase can be seen as restricting or controlling the urge to make "our" existence the very centre of all being. I do not claim at all that people whose language does not emphasize the subject "I" would be devoid of individualism. An individualistic trend or feature is fully present in Estonians, as in Spaniards and persons from other nations. However, the possibilities in a language to accept "otherness" can translate metaphorically into human interaction as a potential broadening of the zone of a dialogue between "I" and "we," on the one hand, and "thou/you/he/she/it/they," on the other.

Especially the most ancient, original words in different languages—not only in Greek or Sanskrit—can contribute to understanding the world around us, and perhaps also suggest some moral tasks not yet achieved by humankind. Thus it is curious that in Estonian the abbreviated form of the personal pronoun "I," *ma*, phonetically resembles another stem-word, "earth": *maa*. That there is a difference in the length of the vowel—in the former, "a" is short, in the latter, it is long—does not exclude the possibility that both words be understood as one and the same reality: I represent a patch of earth, a germ born from it. The earth is the origin of all existence. We cannot discuss the "other" without having a discussing subject. Whatever the shades of difference, we can see the world only through our own eyes, perceiving their bearer as "I," with his/her feet relying on a particular patch of the earth, inseparable from "I." *Ma is maa*.

To explore further this matter of linguistic signs metaphorically translatable into reality: like "I" itself, the most intimate "object" besides the "I" has in Estonian a polysemy. English long ago abandoned the intimate personal pronoun "thou," but it is still widely used in most languages. In Estonian the full form for "thou" is *sina*, but again its abbreviated form, *sa*, is more commonly applied in practice. In parallel with *ma—maa*, *sa* has a phonetic coincidence with *saa*, which means "let thee have!," "thou become!," "thou have!," "thou get!," that is, with imperative forms applied to the intimate personal pronoun "thou."

As in these examples, language can contain metaphorical suggestions of shared being or existence, the willingness of "I" to share the world and his/her life with "thou," or the other.

* * *

Since the last decades of the 20th century, a new broad field in human sciences has emerged, called "gender studies." You may imagine that it has to do with medicine, but it is not so. It is a field populated in its absolute majority by women researchers of culture and literature. It has emerged in the background of democratic processes in Western societies and womankind's general liberation and emancipation, especially after WWII. It is part of a phenomenon that in my opinion can change the course of history more significantly than wars and revolutions waged and made by men in the preceding centuries. Womankind's awakening and its striving to establish its natural rights and its needs is a fully justified reaction to all historical injustice done to womankind by the "leading" gender, man. You, Montaigne, were among the first humanist writers to understand woman's individuality and her deep natural and psychological difference from men, as well as her natural reluctance to submit to man's reason and logic.

Yet in our contemporary gender studies there is an obvious over-optimism as regards womankind's possibilities to reach its final liberation. In fact, such liberation can never become reality, because liberty for both human genders is denied by the very limits of any individual existence as well as by responsibilities that both men and women have to assume in the daily effort to survive in a world in which illnesses, plagues, hunger, wars and natural calamities, despite all advances of science and clever discourses of economists, daily haunt millions of human souls. Let alone the natural environment, which has been destroyed by humans to such an extent that literally no place is left for establishing a "paradise" either for the liberated female-kind or male-kind.

Once again, I find in my native language some signs that could encourage humankind to seek a more balanced and symbiotic course, instead of antagonism between the genders. Romance languages, in which a great number of influential discourses in contemporary gender studies have been created, cannot do without a strict gender division: Words are either masculine or feminine. They seem to have been determined by God, who is definitely masculine. Feminist scholars relying on Romance languages attack God, as *ur*-Male, the original cause of all vices and injustice done to women. God can only be male, because the gender article defines it: *le, el, il*. Even though because of the Christian God's uniqueness the article is mostly omitted in front of his name, he can only be conceived as masculine. Though linguists may not agree, "god" in Old Germanic language sounds very close to "good." Women in our days would definitely reject the idea that all good emanates from a male god.

English is more neutral (and pragmatic). Words' gender does exist in English, but it is revealed by action and background, not by a definite article preceding words. But Estonian, a Finno-Ugric language, differs radically both from Germanic and from Romance languages in that it does not have a linguistic gender category at all. For you, Montaigne, as well as for any other speaker of Romance languages it would seem almost impossible to imagine how a language without gender categories could work. Yet it works, though not without posing problems for a translator of Estonian literary works into a Romance language. Thus for instance if an Estonian writer wishes to include an ambiguity and not to reveal if a character in a novel is male or female, he /she can do it easily, as the personal pronoun *tema* (abbreviated: *ta*) is equally valid for "he" and "she."

Thus in my native language there is an equality between genders. Metaphorically, it reflects a principle of inter-gender equality. Historically, humankind has not achieved such equality, but the radical change from relationships between genders as they have stood in past centuries and as they stand in present-day democratic societies demonstrates eloquently that changes and shifts are possible. You admired indigenous communities of the New World, the American continent, from where Europe in your days received abundant first-hand evidence about the social habits and traditions of Native American peoples. You speak of indigenous tribes whose men were accompanied in their military campaigns by women, a substantial difference in comparison with European practices during most centuries that we know. I too have read from first-hand sources, thus, from the chronicles by your contemporary Spaniards such as Gonzalo Fernández de Oviedo, the author of *La historia general y natural de las Indias*, that in pre-conquest Nicaragua women were the more active in social and political life, while men took care of domestic work …

In contemporary Estonia, a young independent state and nation in Europe, we have not yet lived up to our language in this regard. The traditions of male-dominance are deep, as we inevitably have had to imitate patterns adapted by the major European nations. Our modern state was men-built. Even in the present day political scene men dominate, in contrast with our neighbour Finland whose women have lived for a longer period in democratic conditions and like all Scandinavian women have obtained gender privileges most world communities still lack. In some of the Scandinavian countries, but also in Spain, women have recently become ministers of defense …

* * *

I would like to mention one more way in which language reflects our attitudes to the surrounding world, at the same time providing generic-semantic relations, which could be imagined as models for certain changes and shifts in reality. It is especially important in view of your largest essay, "An Apology for Raymond Sebond." I would call the ideas in that essay a truly revolutionary change in Western philosophy. Exemplifying and generating Sebond's bold assertions in his *Theologia naturalis* about God who has endowed all living beings with soul, you emerge as the first radical critic of anthropocentrism, the historical cornerstone of Western humanity's religion and morals.

You would be pleased to hear that Estonian is among those languages—there may be in the world many others of which I lack knowledge—whose gender systems concur with Sebond's thinking, for which you wrote so extensive an apology.

When I learned English, I was surprised that English could apply to small children, babies, and all the animal species the neutral form of the personal pronoun: "it." Now at the start of the 21st century I have read that this attitude has faced criticism. As the result, these sources say, the English have started to apply "he" and "she" also to children, when their gender is known, and also to domestic animals, pets, whose gender is known to those who speak about them.

Indeed, these advances can be welcomed, but still in general usage animal species are referred to in English as "it." They are depersonalized, reflecting the overwhelming attitude of Western society to animals, birds, fish, insects, etc., as inferior beings, devoid of soul. When I read a recent book by the Estonian thinker Fanny de Sivers, *Jumala loomaaed—tuttav tundmatu maailm* (*God's Zoo—the Known Unknown World*, Tartu, 2010), I started to understand that the Christian church has done much to alienate humanity from other living creatures. During the long history of Western Christianity such an attitude could have left its footprints also in the languages of the leading Christian nations, such as English, especially because its definite articles are not bound to a gender.

In my native Estonian, the language of one of the last European "pagan" nations (forced to Christianity as late as the middle of the 13th century), all living beings, humans—old or young, men, women, children—as well as animals, fish, insects, and birds are designated by means of the personal pronoun *tema* (abbreviated: *ta*), while in the case of things, trees, and plants the neutral form *see* ("it") is used. Thus our language unconsciously generates an understanding that all living creatures are equal before the supreme Creator, *Jumal* (God). The latter, too, is *tema* (ta), though in this case mostly the complete form, *tema*, has preference. Naturally, under the influence of Christian religion, *jumal* is generally conceived as male. How our remotest ancestors conceived *jumal*, whether they imagined the supreme power as male or female or without gender, is unknown.

At least to some extent, my meditations have been influenced by the work of Yuri M. Lotman, a Russian-Jewish cultural scholar who in the 1960s made my hometown Tartu and its university world famous by his semiotic approach to culture. He claimed that natural as well as artificial language systems (including the language of different arts) model reality, each of them in its own particular way. Thus already in his early works he applied the terms "syntagmatic" and "paradigmatic," to contrast regular, more or less rational and rectilinear (syntagmatic) phenomena in arts to unpredictable, sudden, irregular (paradigmatic) appearances.

In his late stage of work (he died in 1993), he was above all fascinated by the unpredictable in culture. He introduced such notions as "leaps" and "explosions," applying them to the most radical revolutions in literature and arts—like the great Renaissance turn in your lifetime, or the Romantic turn, two centuries after your passing away. In his late work, Lotman came very close to the ideas expressed in your *Essays*. He invented the term of "semiosphere," meaning by it the imaginary intersection zone between biosphere and noosphere. The closer culture moves to this border-zone, the more there are premises for "explosions" and "leaps," or turns to radically new qualities in culture. Lotman respected cultural diversity and sought a dialogue, not only between different types of culture, but also between different socio-economical systems.

Yet as Lotman's last important work, the book *Culture and Explosion*, shows, Lotman could not make a final "leap" to the admission of all life as equal in nature. He maintained human superiority and could not conceive the existence of semiosis (or the emergence of new signs) outside human activity. He was sceptical about the idea forwarded in your "An Apology for Raymond Sebond," about animals as having an equal intellectual and creative potential with humans. Thus Lotman came close to abandoning an anthropocentric position, but never did.

Lotman's children and grandchildren have fully merged with the Estonian community and society. He himself—being a child of the Soviet-Russian "empire"—never managed to learn Estonian. Had he learned it, maybe he could have been inspired by Juhan Liiv, the

Estonian poet-philosopher I briefly mentioned, in the context of translation, in my first letter to you. Liiv, whose work I have recently studied in detail, quite certainly never read your *Essays*. However, following his intuition and life experience, without any university studies, despite extreme poverty and fits of mental illness, he reached in all fundamental philosophical questions the same conclusions as you in your *Essays*.

For Liiv, life is a whole. Soul and body are one, inseparable in all living beings. One cannot harm or destroy a part of nature without harming the whole, as well as man's own existence. Therefore, one should have moral responsibility for every particle of nature. It does not concern only individual existence, but also the existence of nationalities and nations, all of whom, big or small, everyone with their individual language, culture, and religion are unique and necessary for life's continuation on the earth. Humanity has no superiority over the rest of living nature. We humans have no right to destroy nature around us, for the sake of our own material welfare and progress.

Knowledge and science are not self-sufficient. By one-sidedly developing them, goodness, moral virtue or love can never be achieved. Senses and feelings are not less important than knowledge or reason. All knowledge is relative. It depends on opinions, which vary from person to person, from one generation to the other. Death puts a limit to the aspirations of science and mind. The primary awareness comes into humans through the senses. They can be mistaken, but by suppressing them by reason, we annihilate sensibility in us and abandon love, the nucleus of all virtue, in all its multiple manifestations. Also in poetry, you cannot create a good poem by mere reasoning, without a flame catching simultaneously your thoughts and senses.

Annex 1

Daniel Defoe: *Robinson Crusoe* (1719)

DANIEL DEFOE WAS SURELY THE first butcher's son to achieve prominence in the wide field of world literature. The next was Franz Kafka, born to the family of a butcher in Prague, at the end of the 19th century. Both men are characterized by a special sensibility, attentive to what extends beyond a human person's private life. Both took painfully to heart society that surrounds us all from birth and that makes many of us evil and cruel. For a moral vivisection of society, both applied to society one of its own predominant languages: Kafka wrote in a dry style of officials, in the language of bureaucracy, while Defoe loaded his novels with calculations, numbers and facts, to become a forerunner of factual-testimonial literature of the second half of the 20th century (Truman Capote, Miguel Barnet, and others).

New interest in life-stories, in nonfiction, departs from feminist gender studies of the end of the 20th century. Reading Defoe's *Robinson Crusoe* should make explicit the advantages that the imaginary world of a writer has over factual life-stories, attached to the real world and thus inevitably devoid of broader philosophical perspectives or generalizations. The hope that cultural scholars by their discussions *a posteriori* will discern in biographies robust philosophy is not great at all. It will in any case remain in the narrow circles of scholars, without exercising on society as a whole the curing influence that can often be found in good literary works.

Defoe's own life-story does not include travels beyond Europe. In any case he had never been on an island near the Venezuelan coast where he destined his imaginary character Robinson Crusoe to fight for survival and meditate about existence, nor on the Chilean island in the Juan Fernandez Archipelago, now bearing the name of Robinson Crusoe.

Another island of the same archipelago is Alexander Selkirk. It hides the most important source for *Robinson Crusoe*. Selkirk was a seaman who in 1704 quarrelled with the captain of his ship and remained of his own free will on the islands of Juan Fernandez. For Defoe, it was just the starting point. He did not fall prisoner to facts. His Robinson spent on his island twenty-seven years—a time lapse large enough to bring some clarity to his own self.

A lonely island is not the same as a prison; its signs are different. The French philosopher Jean-Jacques Rousseau gave to Émile, the main character of his large pedagogical treatise bearing the same name, only two books to be read, the Bible and *Robinson Crusoe*. He felt very enthusiastic about Defoe's idea of describing his Robinson's actions and adventures amid pure nature, away from a perverted society. It was near to his heart that Defoe let his Robinson—who until finding himself on the island had been superficial, clinging to earthy greed—discover in his suffering God and find a spiritual ground for his existence.

Nature, faith, and such work as has no goal of profit make Defoe's Robinson and Rousseau's Émile, hand in hand, truly human persons. Shades of differences still remain. Robinson had an obscure idea of cannibals being also God's creation. Friday became his faithful companion, almost a friend. Yet on the background of the ever more rapid expansion of Europe's colonial possessions, Robinson never abandoned the posture of a lord, superior to "savages."

Rousseau went much further: all human beings, all races are equal. There are no signs that the 21st-century world stands ready to accept his conclusions. If ears willing to listen to Robinson's cry of worry in his insular solitude could be found, at least for the time being, it would not be bad at all.

LETTER 3

NOW I HAVE BEEN FOR nearly a week here in Rhodes. The sky is immutably blue, and winds blow immutably. In my homeland, Estonia, November is the gloomiest month. Mostly it is without snow, but it is cold, rainy, cloudy, dark and windy. A year ago rough cold weather settled in right from the first days of November, with early snow and temperatures some ten degrees below zero, so that snow did not melt but stayed through the winter, until March. On the average, earth in Estonia remains frozen, apparently dead, during four or five months of a year.

This morning I put my finger haphazardly onto notes taken while reading your *Essays*. The line happened to be a quotation: "The wisest man that ever was, when asked what he knew, replied that the one thing he did know was that he knew nothing." ("An Apology for Raymond Sebond," CE 5581.) You had in mind Socrates. Indeed, one of the phrases posterity has highlighted as an essence of your own philosophy is your question: "Que jais-je?" It shows your scepticism, which replicates Socrates' doubt.

Greece is generally considered the cradle of Western philosophy. Indeed, the climate which for a greater part of the year is warm or moderate, apparently favours thinking. One cannot think for long in

---

1   Here and in the following, CE = Michel de Montaigne, *The Complete Essays*. Translated and edited with an Introduction and Notes by M.A. Schreech. London: Penguin Books, 2003.

a room with a temperature near freezing. It is probably a legend, but different sources claim that René Descartes, your compatriot, who half a century after your death wrote his influential book *Discours de la méthode*, conceived his theory while spending a cold morning in a large heated oven, in 1619 on his army duty at Ulm. With Descartes, the Modern Era (as we now call it) established its philosophical mainstream, based fundamentally on strict logic and reason. It revived the ancient tradition represented above all by Aristotle.

Now here comes my doubt. While cold definitely curbs any flow of thought, does not steady warmth granted by nature lead thought to run in the channels of our brains too fluently, becoming a kind of instinctive self-enjoyment in those endowed by nature with spacious brain channels? Thought in such conditions perceives no significant exterior obstacles, so it tends to build up ever more extensive chains of reasoning, creating an illusion that definite knowledge can be achieved.

You have given one of your essays the title "To philosophize is to learn how to die." I suspect philosophers working in warmth or steadily favourable condition follow just the opposite principle: to philosophize means to learn to forget death. As for myself, I can hardly forget it, because I surely cannot finish my planned cycle of essays while staying here in Rhodes writers' centre. In three weeks' time I will return to the harsh winter and cold of my country. Travel and a change of surroundings, insofar as they allow one to experience the relativity of existence, its constantly changing interior weather, to let the senses open to both warmth and cold, definitely do good to one's thinking capacity.

One of your phrases has especially deeply settled in my memory: "Frequent commerce with the world can be an astonishing source of light for a man's judgment" ("On Educating Children," CE 176). I too think that only through the experience of variety and difference, as well as pain and difficulty, can reason avoid self-admiration, vanity and arrogance, by which it is constantly haunted, and reach some clarity, even if illumination is not definite.

You call Socrates the wisest man who has ever lived and fully share the philosophy contained in his famous phrase. However, one has to admit that we really do not know much about Socrates. Thus we do not know to what extent the image of Socrates, provided by the work of Plato, corresponds to reality. We do not know who really wished to banish poets from the ideal Republic, Socrates or Plato. If Socrates is but Plato's fiction, then Plato himself has committed the sin of creating an illusion or a lie, of which he accused poets. I will not go into the details of this discussion. More can be found in a number of scholarly books on the topic. However, from my initial readings of Plato I have the impression that his so-called idealism has to do not only with exiling poets, but with an inherent tendency to subordinate the senses to reason and logic.

His attacks on poetry might have had in their background on the one hand the fact that from the most ancient times, poetry has always been created not only by a tiny minority of really great poets, but also by a great number of mediocre or simply bad poets. The work of the latter, which nonetheless has always found its keen admirers, has created a general impression of poetry as something vain and superficial.

On the other hand, despite the above criticisms of Plato as an earnest truth-seeker, he might have also intuitively grasped the power and magic of great poetry, suspecting it as a rival to philosophy, especially because outstanding poets have always had a much wider acceptance in society than those philosophers who, like scientists, seek the truth of reason and logic. We know nothing of Plato's intimate background. We do not know anything about Plato's love, and we do not know if he himself ever tried to write poems. Maybe he failed in both, thus being left with a grudge against those who, on the contrary, had luck in love and were successful in creating talented poetry? Why should we think that the greatest philosophers or scientists are invulnerable in such matters? Are they not humans like the rest of us?

Envy, one of the deepest human sentiments, goes back to the most ancient times human memory can reach. The Biblical story of Cain and Abel exemplifies it magnificently. It has been turned into a fascinating short novel, *Abel Sánchez. Historia de una pasión*, by Miguel de Unamuno, a Spanish writer and philosopher of Basque origin, who wrote his best-known essays and novels at the start of the 20th century. He was born in 1864, the same year as our Estonian poet-philosopher Juhan Liiv. Among the great number of Western philosophers who have lived and written since your lifetime, Unamuno belonged to the few who dared to go beyond, and to oppose, the rationalistically oriented mainstream. He asserted the same ideas that can be found in your essays and in Liiv's poetic images. Reason or intellect does not represent man as a whole. On the contrary, man's deeper essence is revealed in his feelings and passions. They constitute his "intra-existence" and form his "intra-history."

Now I am at pains, using English "he" and "man" but wanting to speak of humans in general. I am happy that at least I can think freely of that unity between man and woman in my language, Estonian, which has in its vocabulary a middle term, *inimene*, that includes no shade of "man" (*mees*) or "woman" (*naine*).

Unamuno tells in his novel a story of two friends, a scientist (medical doctor) and an artist. Although the scientist (Joaquín) is a serious and earnest man, a truth-seeker, the world applauds instead Abel, a light-minded and superficial artist, who nevertheless has much more luck with women than Joaquín and is also loved by Joaquín's grandson. Joaquín cannot suppress his *ur*-passion, envy, and the story ends in tragedy.

Unamuno himself wrote poetry, too. In that genre his achievements cannot be compared with those of such truly great poets of his generation as the Spaniards Antonio Machado and Juan Ramón Jiménez, or our Estonian Juhan Liiv. In his poetry Unamuno had the tendency to foreground his ideas. German has a special term for ideologically-driven literature: *Tendenzliteratur, Tendenzdichtung*.

One of the giants of German literature, the poet and dramatist Friedrich Schiller, who had also a keen mind for criticism, called it somewhat paradoxically "sentimental poetry," in the sense that a poet in such a work does not so much imitate nature as make stand forth his ideas, his conception or philosophy. Schiller was well aware that he himself was inclined in his poems to such "sentimentality." However, he was generous enough to appreciate fully the other tendency that he called "naive poetry." He found that, more than he himself, his friend and fellow-writer Johann Wolfgang von Goethe—mainly known to literary posterity for *Faust*, a philosophical-dramatic poem—exemplified the trend of "naive poetry," based on imitation of nature, rather than assertion of ideas.

Whatever their inclination and particular emphasis, I can hardly think of any truly great author in the field of literature who would not have cared for poetry. The source of their greatness is that in their work they combined philosophy with an original poetic image. Exterior forms hardly matter. In the 17th century, verse forms still dominated most literary genres. Thus Shakespeare and Calderón, as well as other great dramatic authors of the 17th century, wrote their dramas predominantly in verse. Miguel de Cervantes was the first to write a great work of prose fiction in which philosophy and poetic image merge, to form a magnificent symbiosis. Cervantes wrote poetry too, but it does not have the brilliance of his great "poem in prose," the novel *Don Quixote*. Also, in the second half of the 20th century the Colombian Gabriel García Márquez, a highly talented prose writer, who never published poems, owed the enormous success of his novel *Cien años de soledad* (*One Hundred Years of Solitude*) to poetic imagery combined with his mature philosophy of life. His prose fiction represents at the same time a real and a fantastic world; it is full of poetic and lyrical images, myths and magic.

You confess that you yourself failed to write poems. Greatness of mind, in my opinion, is revealed above all in one's capacity to respect the other. Throughout your work you reiterate your deepest respect for poetic creation. You frequently quote verse lines and poems, to expose and support your own thoughts.

Here lies the difference. Often those who have tried to debut as poets, but have failed, take up writing criticism. As critics, they reveal their hostility to poetic spirit, as if trying to avenge their own failure as poets. It is hard for me to believe that Plato could have belonged to that guild of extremely narrow-minded persons, though I confess that his hostility to poetry makes me doubt the breadth of his spirit.

You probably would have expected me to say: "the breadth of his mind." No, I quite consciously said "spirit." It is another key notion. In applying it, different nations in their languages reflect something of dominant attitudes influencing people's opinions. Plato's mind was great, but his spirit was narrow. Or maybe I am mistaken? Perhaps mind and spirit are inseparable, as body and soul, and there cannot be mental greatness without spiritual breadth? Indeed, for me, since I advocate a symbiotic principle, their union would be most desirable.

However, in practice I observe that spirit and mind have been torn apart from each other. Even sadder, mind has been identified with reason and intellect, treated as self-sufficient, without need of spirit. Today's hard sciences, the "pure" reign of mind, intellect, and reason, supported by economic-political power structures and the dominant systems of education, have assumed an utterly arrogant position, looking down at humanities, culture, and literary-artistic creation—the field of spirit and spiritual values—as something inferior, or as mere entertainment.

* * *

In the Europe of my days, the idea of a European empire has been resuscitated. The European Union, formed after WWII, can be seen as an offshoot of the major empires Europe has had in the past, especially the Holy Roman Empire, which before you were born, was renamed the Holy Roman Empire of the German Nation. It lasted until 1806. It had in its structure the notion of "holy," implying that the church occupied a preeminent role in it and that spiritual values, at least officially, were considered of primary importance. The present-day European Union, on the contrary, was from the very beginning conceived as a political-economic entity, to defend the economic interests of the Western European countries relying politically on a democratic system.

As soon as Spain, Portugal, and Greece got rid of their dictators, they too were admitted to the European Union. After a major political-social earthquake in Eastern Europe, the collapse of the Soviet-Russian empire (USSR, or the Union of the Socialist Soviet Republics, as it was officially called), some of its former member republics, and more concretely, the three East-Baltic nations, Estonia, Latvia, and Lithuania, along with most East-European countries, formerly belonging to the "socialist camp," were admitted to the European Union.

Where is the church, you may ask? Yes, it is still here. Also, the Pope has his residence in Rome. However, religious life is in clear decline, since rough materialistic values dominate in all modern societies, even in those with long religious traditions, such as Spain, Portugal, and Italy. I say nothing of my homeland, Estonia. With a population of just slightly above one million, it has been easily manipulated by predominant ideological currents coming from major nations. As Estonians were turned to Christian religion by force, mainly by the German knights and clergyman, and at the same time were kept as serfs under the dominance of German landlords, it is but natural that Christian feeling could not take deeper root in my ancestors. The Russian-Soviet empire to which Estonia was annexed for the major part of the second half of the 20th century denied any religion and tried to show itself as a state whose official philosophy was based on atheism and materialism.

In fact, the Soviet-Russian empire, at least in its ascending phase, was a fanatically religious state—its religion was dogmatic communism. Despite its officially claimed materialism, it was fiercely opposed to capitalism.

Now as we became integrated into the Western capitalist system and its values, it is not difficult to understand that the feigned or (platonically) idealized materialism of the former USSR was precipitously replaced by real materialism, in which spiritual values either had been abandoned or were seen as something of secondary importance. At least from the start of the 20th century, the world's mightiest super-power has been the United States, built up mainly by the protestant middle class who migrated or fled to America since the 17th century. The U.S. has come to symbolize a society based on the principle of money and business, that is, rough materialistic values and attitudes.

All European states have a ministry of culture, but the U.S. does not have one. In all European states capital punishment of criminals have been abolished, as something contrary to the spirit of democracy and humanness, yet in many states of the U.S. capital punishment in its different forms is still being practiced. Thus the U.S., initially a vast "periphery" of Europe, retains some of the wild habits practiced today mainly by Asian or African nations, governed by dictators or military regimes. (The latter, luckily, have started to reveal signs of weakness, as some of the Arab-language countries, such as Libya, have been liberated from their dictators.)

Another major communist superpower after WWII, China, has in recent decades, after Mao Zedong's harsh and dogmatized ideological line, become a capitalist market economy. It is one of the paradoxes at the start of the 21st century: Communist ideology has combined in China with capitalist economy. It may give the impression of an apparently attractive symbiosis, but I am afraid it can only work in some Eastern countries, where despite all dogmatisms there survive strong traditions of ancient culture, saturated with moral values.

In producing paradoxes and surprises, "periphery" can by far exceed "centres"—as Yuri Lotman has taught us. It may be due to its remote peripheral past that the U.S., in parallel with its overwhelming business spirit, still keeps alive some oases of poetic spirit, not only as the heritage of the brightest writers of Britain, but also as the legacy of the major knights of the spirit of North America itself. I think above all of the poet Walt Whitman, whose powerful free-verse songs exalting the unity of man and woman, nations and races, in equal rights, as well as humankind's unity with nature and soul's unity with body would have made you quite surely enthusiastic about the greatness of America's beginnings.

I myself enjoyed some of America's generosity. The Fulbright scholarships awarded to university professors around the world are not meant only for hard scientists, but also for people working in humanities and arts. Not many years ago America awarded me a Fulbright scholarship for editing and translating a major anthology of American poetry in Estonian translation. I cannot imagine that the same could have happened in Europe, where sciences are strictly separated from humanities and arts. The other example of peripheral legacy still manifesting itself on the American continent is the World Council of Culture, with its headquarters in Mexico. Every year its international board awards a scientist and an artist a prize. It is not as prestigious as the Nobel Prize, founded by the Swedish chemist and armaments manufacturer Alfred Nobel at the end of the 19th century, but still, world scientists consider it a high honour to be brought forth by the WCC.

In the background of the brutal dominance of hard sciences over humanities, it is all but habitual that an international organization, having "culture" on its official label, should give one of its two annual awards to men of hard sciences, those who in our days often do not want to know anything at all about culture and cultural-creative activity ...

* * *

The paradox, however, can be explained quite easily in the background of the tradition formed in Europe in the 18th century. We call it the Enlightenment. Some of the leading spirits and men of letters of that period, notably Voltaire and the authors of the French Encyclopaedia (especially Diderot) imagined culture and civilization as a unity. The spirit of unity still prevailed during the Romantic era, though a schism between the two gradually started to emerge. With the scientific and technological revolution of the second half of the 19th century, the interrelationship between culture and science changed at the very root.

The Spanish philosopher José Ortega y Gasset was among the first to analyze in his essays at the start of the 20th century the ever more visible split between culture and civilization, the first being promoted by arts and humanities, and the latter, by science and technology. In his influential essay *La rebelión de las masas* (*The Revolt of the Masses*), Ortega y Gasset includes in the category of "mass man" specialized scientists and technologists, doctors, engineers, and so on, who do have no need of culture, but earn their livings by specialized skills. They become a mass without any broader social awareness, thus a mass that can be easily manipulated by political-economical power.

On this background of historical developments, let me return to the linguistic signs of "spirit" and "spiritual" on the one hand, and "mind" and "mental" on the other. "Intellect" and "reason" belong to the same complex. Often they have been seen as identical. At one stage of his activity, which he definitely imagined as scientific, Yuri Lotman defined culture as "collective intellect." In one of his publications, he even called it "collective reason." Such a definition would have some sense, if we identify culture with science, as was done in the 18th-century Enlightenment and still, to some extent, in the 19th century.

Because Lotman at that time was actively researching the structures of artificial intellect and the interrelations between the cerebral hemispheres, such applications of "intellect" and "reason" are understandable. Besides, one should not ignore the historical-political condition of Lotman's work. His semiotic research was always followed with suspicion on the part of the official Soviet-Russian authorities. Even the term "semiotics" itself had to be camouflaged to some extent. At the same time "reason" was one of the positive key signs in the eyes of the official ideologists. Science enjoyed a privileged position in the Soviet-Russian system, in direct opposition to philosophy, of which only the Marxist-materialistic line was considered correct and "objective." Any freer thinking was not tolerated at all.

In gradually more liberal conditions, Lotman never returned to the terms of "collective intellect" or "collective reason." Instead he invented the notion of "semiosphere," which was much broader in its meaning than "intellect / reason." (The latter, according to Lotman, forms the basis of "noosphere.") Lotman definitely abandoned in his later research the "noospheric"-structuralist line and was, instead, far more interested in what happened in the "semiosphere," the imaginary border zone between "biosphere" and "noosphere." From "intellect / reason" he now shifted to the far more complex philosophical ground on which "mind" and "spirit" entered into a most complicated relationship. Lotman was now fascinated by the "unpredictable," "irrational," "spiritual," sensorial-sexual, etc. By that time he certainly realized that all of them had a part in cultural creation and arts, which in contrast to science, can hardly be conceived by purely mental efforts.

There is an obvious "term shortage" in a number of languages of bigger nations. Such a shortage is especially revealed in translation. In the course of historical developments some notions have been modified and some have fallen out of use. Paradoxically, a small peripheral language, like Estonian, though definitely influenced by neighbouring big nations' languages (in our case, German and Russian especially) has managed to conserve and develop notions that enable the reflection of realities more precisely than some of the Indo-European languages of the biggest nations.

To give you some examples, let me first mention a poem by the great English romantic poet Percy Bysshe Shelley, entitled "A Hymn to Intellectual Beauty." In his young days Shelley was fiercely opposed to the Christian God and the church. He tried to replace God by a confluence of natural deities, to construct a pantheon that would be higher than Christian God. In his long dramatic poem *The Revolt of Islam* he, however, was not able to conceive, instead of Dante's Empyrean (the abode of Christian God), any other place than the Temple of the Spirit. The souls of the two young lovers, executed by tyrants, ascend in the final episode of Shelley's poem to the Temple of the Spirit.

(In the same period, Shelley translated from Spanish into English *El mágico prodigioso*, a drama written by Pedro Calderón de la Barca, one of the greatest dramatic poets of the 17th century Baroque era. It is a paradox in itself, not insignificant. Shelley followed the example of

Calderón, who is known as a thoroughly Catholic poet. In Calderón's drama, the souls of the executed lovers ascend to Heaven, the Home of Christian God.) Thus Shelley admitted spirit as the highest and absolute reality.

However, in "A Hymn to Intellectual Beauty" Shelley apparently ran into trouble while trying to find a proper adjective. He could not use "spiritual" (instead of "intellectual"), because "spiritual" was (and is still) a key notion in the Christian church. "Spirituality" and "spiritual," as generally conceived, belong to the domain of clergymen and priests, the "spiritual people."

So Shelley used instead the term "intellectual."

He certainly could not resort to "rational," because "rational" and "reasonable" are, far more directly than "intellectual," related to calculation and measuring, the very basis of business life in the world. If I buy something at "reasonable" price, I make some brain operations of calculation, finding out that the price is not too high and I can afford to buy the item. "Rational" in its turn has come to denote the pragmatically most purposeful action. Thus it is also based on calculation. Neither has to do with the notion of "spiritual." By contrast, "intellectual" leaves more space to the wider notion of "mind," even though "mental," too, first and foremost has been understood as connected with human brain or cerebral activity.

The above-mentioned Spanish philosopher Ortega y Gasset has given "intellectuality" an important shade, associating it with its etymological stem in Latin, "eligere" (to choose) and has demonstrated that the adjective "elegant" derives from the same stem ... "Intelligent" means "elegant." Thus we enter the realm of artistic creation and beauty, which certainly was closest to Shelley's dedication. It explains the combination of "intellectual beauty," in the title of his poem.

It is not by chance that in our day "intellectuals" are identified more often than not with writers and philosophers, especially philosophically-minded and socially-oriented writers, like you, rather than with scientists or technically specialized people. Naturally, there are exceptions. Scientists who have interested themselves in broader social and cultural processes have been situated in our day under the sign of "intellectuals."

In German, Shelley's "intellectual" has been translated as *geistliche*. Thus the German language, to a greater extent than English, provides a link between the stem noun (*Geist*—Spirit) and its adjectival application. It is the same in Estonian. "Spirit" is *vaim* and "spiritual" is *vaimne*. However, as opposed to both German and Russian (дух— spirit; духовный—spiritual), in Estonian we differentiate between *vaimne* and *vaimulik*, the former coinciding with spiritual-mental, and the latter, unambiguously, with the notion of "religious," because the noun *vaimulik* means "religious man," "clergyman." Had Shelley written in Estonian, he would have had little hesitation: His choice would have been *vaimne*.

The same is true of a collection of articles by Lotman in English translation. Its title is *The Universe of the Mind*. "Mind" is definitely a proper word in English translation. It refers to human cerebral activity in the broadest sense. But to translate it into German or Russian would be problematic. The meaning would shift either too directly into the realm of "reason / intellect" or to the "spiritual" field. In German the closest term would be "Sinn," but it tends to denote a product of mind, not mind itself. In Russian, English "mind" does not have a good equivalent either. If one translates it "смысл" (perhaps closest to German "Sinn"), the meaning drifts farther away from "mind."

Once again, the advantage of my native Estonian is that we can easily apply here, as in the case of Shelley's "intellectual," either the noun *vaim* or the adjective *vaimne*. Our main Estonian advocate of Shelley's poetry, Ants Oras, a leading pre-war intellectual, translated the title "Hümn vaimsele ilule," thus using the adjective *vaimne*. Also, Lotman's *The Universe of the Mind* would most probably translate as *vaimne maailm* or, even better, *vaimumaailm* (*vaim* = spirit, *maailm* = world, universe). As you see, once again we have to return to "spirit"—something that had a special accent in Lotman's late and most mature work.

Yet I will not idealize my native "peripheral" Estonian. It is true that at times our language reveals a surprising flexibility. However, especially in the use of the derivate of *vaim* (spirit, *Geist,* дух, absolutely essential when discoursing on matters of philosophy and artistic creation and, culture, as a whole), I feel its insufficiency. Thus probably under the influence of languages of bigger nations, *vaimne* has shifted in Estonian, too, close to "mental" (cerebral, brain-produced), while abandoning "spiritual" which in English overlaps with the semantic area connected with "soul."

Thus when speaking about the goal of literature or creative arts, the term "mental" (*vaimne*) is not exhaustive. I would rather use in this case a borrowed foreign word, *spirituaalne* (spiritual), which, as applied in Estonian, does not belong so exclusively to the domain of religion, as in English, but sounds as a kind of mixture or symbiosis of "soul" (which in English, strangely enough, does not have its adjectival derivate), "heart," and "mind."

Thus I have applied in such a context a compound adjective *hinge-lis-vaimne*. *Hing* is "soul" in Estonian, while *hingeline* is its adjectival derivate. Only a narrow margin has been reserved for it in the vocabulary of the rationally-inclined mainstream Western philosophy. It can be sought in great literary and artistic creation, with literature ever in its vanguard, because "soul" or "heart" and feelings are not alone there, but (more powerfully than in any other field of culture) overlap, in a symbiotic interrelationship, with "mind."

Annex 2

Miguel de Cervantes: *The Ingenious Gentleman Don Quixote of La Mancha* (1605–1615)

IN ONE OF HIS NEWSPAPER articles, the late Estonian writer Mati Unt mentioned in passing that Cervantes' *Don Quixote* was too rationalistic for his taste. Many thoughts persist in this world, without any chance given to us to ask their authors what they really meant. Such thoughts left to posterity by Cervantes are much more numerous than those to be found in the writing of Mati Unt or of the Argentine Jorge Luis Borges, one of the greatest modern masters of ludic-intellectual prose. One of his stories, written in the 1940s, is entitled "Pierre Menard, Author of the *Quixote*." It has ever intrigued and inspired people engaged in interpreting literature and culture. The main character of the story has become famous for writing a new *Don Quixote* that word by word coincides with Cervantes' original novel.

There is room enough in Cervantes for both Unt and Borges. The Basque writer-philosopher Miguel de Unamuno baptized Don Quixote as the Spanish Christ, but long before Unamuno Cervantes' hero had become a myth whose significance is not limited to Spain. The myth-creating mechanism is never simple. In the history of the Western novel no other author has managed to repeat what Cervantes did, even though he has inspired a number of writers, including the English Laurence Sterne and Unamuno himself.

Cervantes managed to create an illusion of a total coincidence of myth and history. Just as the New Testament reproduces Christ's life in four different versions, Cervantes makes the reader believe that there exist several versions about the adventure of Don Quixote and Sancho Panza, the most important among them belonging to the Arab chronicler Cide Hamete Benengeli. Cervantes reduces his own role to merely transmitting the translation in Spanish of Hamete Benengeli's story. Thus we see that in its very germ myth is transferred from West to East; it transcends "self" to embrace the "other." Cervantes denies his role as author, to turn his book into a myth, a reality set free from history's bonds, to be experienced and (re)produced by any reader in his / her own particular rights.

Life with its mess of accidents predicts fates. If Cervantes could have written his book so to say in one piece and at a stretch, he probably would not have achieved the magic effect of merging myth with history. However, his life was tough. He had to earn his living as a collector of revenues and commissary of the Spanish fleet. Neither the Nobel Prize nor the Cervantes Prize, which in the 20th century have eased the material aspect of life of some elderly writers, had been founded yet. It took Cervantes ten years before he could start to write a continuation to Part One of *Don Quixote*. Copyright laws defending authors of literary works did not exist as yet. In the meantime a writer hiding behind Avellaneda's pseudonym wrote a false *Don Quixote*. Cervantes had to defend himself against crib.

Cervantes turned *Don Quixote* into a source of "magic realism" in literature, as he made Don Quixote and Sancho Panza, at the start of Part Two of the novel read and discuss the novel written about their adventures by Cervantes and Avellaneda, the work which originally may have been written in the Arabic language … Metafiction is one of the much employed terms in postmodern vocabulary; Cervantes' *Don Quixote* would be a postmodern novel par excellence. However, returning to the doubt about its rationalism, mentioned in the first passage of my present writing, I would call *Don*

Quixote sur-rationalistic in the sense that here we do not have to do simply with reason, but with divine creative reason. Only such could set the adventures of a couple of madmen, the wandering knight Don Quixote and his squire Sancho Panza, on a fully real historical land-scape and turn the mistress of the whole adventure and the novel, Dulcinea, "invisible," so that she by the special force of her "bodiless" faculty could incarnate that germ, love, that has always moved in their depth myths and history.

LETTER 4

PHILOSOPHY PRETENDS TO BE THE quintessence of wisdom. Knowledge has become the domain of science, so philosophy obviously has to adhere to wisdom, in fulfillment of its original linguistic sign, *sophia*, not *gnosis* nor *episteme*. Philosophy would have little purpose as a sub-species of science. However, if it aspires to be something more general than specialized science, it inevitably has to look for union with poetry and literature, in the broadest sense, because literature, too, has ever striven in its greatest works to accumulate, generate, and manifest wisdom. The accent may differ, but the goal is the same. You have wonderfully resumed the essence of philosophy: its final purpose is virtue ("On Educating Children").

Alfred Nobel, the Swedish scientist and industrialist who in his will established from the start of the 20th century the world's most prestigious prize not only for sciences, but also for literature, wanted the prize to be given for literary works of idealistic inclination. I think Nobel did grasp one essence of all literary creation. If it loses its aspiration to originality and abandons the idea of virtue in the spiritual sense, it indeed becomes mere entertainment for the masses, thus indirectly or directly favouring corruption and the spread of evil. At the same time neither philosophy nor literature can become a set of moral commandments. They should not simplify or schematize reality, but without losing sight of virtue explain reality in all its complexity.

While philosophy operates with ideas and concepts, the primary attributes of literary creation are senses and feelings. All good literature includes a great variety of thoughts and ideas, but these would hardly work if they were not intrinsically intertwined with the substance that is called *psyche*. Great literature has always tried to express the human soul. Pedro Calderón has in one of his dramatic works a beautiful and poetical phrase, full of wisdom: "Love in me has been my soul." Great literature can hardly be conceived beyond love—whatever its shades or aspects.

Love cannot be separated from senses and feelings. If science and an important part of philosophy have consciously avoided their "contamination" by the irrational in ourselves (passions, sensual-sexual instincts) and maintained an "objective" distance from reality, literature, on the contrary, works deep in the reality in which the human appears as a whole—body and soul, the biological-sexual and the rational-moral in their closest union.

I would call it the origin of knowing the "other." Still, I should correct myself at the very start. I must refer to something that cannot be ignored, if we are to talk seriously about the "other." To know the other is hardly sufficient. We must feel and sense the other. In Estonian as well as in English, Russian, and German, "knowing" is directly linked with "knowledge." However, in Estonian there are two ways of speaking about somebody who is not "I" or "we." I can say either *tean teda* (I know him/her) or *tunnen teda* (literally: I feel him/her).

The first names a far more superficial relation: I know, let us say, former U.S. President Obama, German Chancellor Merkel, or any other of whom I may have some knowledge. It means I have heard of or seen them from a distance. If I say *tunnen teda* (I feel him/her), though, it refers to a much more intimate relationship. In that case he/she has had direct contact with me; we have "felt" or "touched" each other, been in a bodily contact (not implying sexual intercourse, but not excluding it). It simply means we are friends or we are quite closely acquainted.

While science and mainstream Western philosophy have been based on knowing and knowledge, literature's great advantage is that it can make one "feel" the "other," lead to a different, deeper, more

intimate knowledge, a genuine premise of establishing a relationship of dialogue or at least certain mutual understanding. The purer
knowledge (the less contaminated by feelings and senses), the more
it leads to a separation, an apartheid, an illusion of self-sufficiency.
Hard sciences in my days have become absolutely inaccessible to
non-scientists. They have built up a huge anonymous complex of
knowledge which even the politicians and the official structures (like
"ethics commissions," as they are called) often do not manage to keep
under control.

All anonymity favours corruption. Big schemes of fraud and
fraudulent business are hidden behind the apparently noble goals of
"humanity's progress," toward which science has generally been considered as a major vehicle. It sounds almost like a joke, but recently
a former head of one the "ethics commissions" on medical science in
Estonia was prosecuted, accused of conducting, with another medical
doctor, officially forbidden experiments on humans.

Scientists today feel offended if political and moral institutions
try to hold them back from developing gene technologies, by which
they promise to take humankind to a new paradise, free of any signs
of Christianity or any other religion which still tries to propagate
moral principles.

Like science, modern philosophy has been created in a language
practically inaccessible to laypersons. Even people well educated in
humanities may have a considerable difficulty in understanding what
people working in the field of "philosophical sciences" want to say.
You, Montaigne, strongly criticized this tendency in your contemporary philosophy. Since then, however, it has only become deeper.
Already a century ago Ortega y Gasset, the Spanish philosopher well
informed in German classical philosophy, spoke of Paris as the "capital of charlatans."

Indeed, some philosophers, your fellow-countrymen, who created their major work in the 1970s and 80s, have revived the *langage
précieux* that was popular in the aristocratic salons of Paris at the start
of the 17th century. The main creed of these philosophers is that by

sophisticated language exercises, which they call "discourses," new meanings can be discovered. They become voluntary prisoners of language. Instead of producing new ideas their main energy is wasted on elaborating some quite trivial ideas, which really should be obvious to any more or less intelligent person. After you, the same tendency in French philosophy was wittily satirized by Molière, perhaps one of the greatest European playwrights of the neoclassical era immediately following the Renaissance.

Still, the trend continues, because it seems to nest deep in human nature. Its *ur*-instinct seeks comfort by forgetting about reality, driving away its sadness or reviving the "golden age," one's childhood, by playing with words and notions, instead of dolls.

Molière in his comedies mocked philosophers of his time, but even more severely mocked men and women of letters, who having come under the spell of science, tried to introduce into literature an extremely complicated system of metaphoric language, understandable only for a few. It was not a phenomenon exclusive to French salons. One of the pioneering writers of this fashion was the Italian Giambattista Marino, who spent a significant part of his life in Paris. There he completed his bulky poem *Adonis*, seen by posterity as the climactic work of his mannerism. In Spain, Luis de Góngora, a priest by profession, wrote even earlier than Marino an extensive two-part poem, *Soledades*, applying a hermetic style, full of complicated mythical allusions and highly elaborated metaphors. His style, akin to mannerism, came to be known as "cultism" or also—as derived from his name—"gongorism."

Góngora was vigorously attacked and ridiculed by Francisco de Quevedo, another giant of Spanish "Golden Age" (*Siglo de Oro*) literature. However, at the start of the 20th century, an influential Spanish movement of poets, known as "Generación del '27" revived Góngora's poetic heritage. The most famous poet of that "generation," Federico García Lorca, perhaps one of Europe's greatest natural talents in poetry of all times—with a special sensibility for metaphoric expression—highly praised Góngora's art, which by the way had been despised by two preceding centuries. More or less similar is the fate of John Donne in English literature.

He developed in his poems a special conceptualized metaphysical style, the opposite of the more direct expression of feelings in the poems and dramatic work of William Shakespeare, one of the greatest poets and playwrights the world has known. Donne, too, was largely neglected during the 18th and 19th centuries. However, at the start of the 20th century, with the rise of the so-called modernist movement in literature and arts, Donne became one of the models for another principal European 20th-century poet, the American-English T.S. Eliot, in whose work elaborate mythical and scholarly references were combined with sometimes even coarse fragments or scenes from everyday life and intimately personal experiences.

Yet the poetics of the Andalusian García Lorca and the Anglo-American T.S. Eliot, both indebted to the metaphoric art and language sensibility of the times of Mannerism and Baroque, overlap only in part. The former created sensual images, in which his telluric-existential philosophy can only be grasped by intuition. You either like and feel the essence of such poetry—its impact on you is direct—or you cannot grasp it, because you do not have the sensibility for it. Even if you find out background details, these do not diminish or amplify the effect of a poem. In Eliot's poetry, on the contrary, there is a strong tendency towards scholarly expression. His images are mostly based on allusions inspired by literature or episodes of his personal life. So, to grasp in its totality the sense of Eliot's chef-d'oeuvre, *The Waste Land*, the poet himself has had to provide notes, an extensive apparatus that in its turn has been impressively enlarged and complemented by scholarly researchers.

The only conclusion one can draw from these examples is that literature, though bound to senses and language, has always oscillated between two trends, revealing now a more direct, now a more metaphorical expression. Often these trends overlap. The more literature tends to one extreme of a trend, the more likely that it has come close to exhausting its possibilities. The metaphors and the images of

García Lorca or, in our Estonian case, of Juhan Liiv, are powerful in their impact, because they have a sound philosophical basis. On the contrary, the weakness of the greater part of symbolist-impressionist poets, highly fashionable at the end of the 19th century and the start of the 20th century, is that they seldom rely on their own original philosophy.

When some poets of the same generation (thus, the famous Chilean Pablo Neruda or the Spaniard Rafael Alberti) tried in the socially oriented part of their poetic work to replace philosophy with political ideology, the result was a failure. Poetry cannot rely on bare or direct expression of ideas, and political ideas, perpetuated by power structures in their immediate interests, seldom serve for poetry. It is really miserable and sad for a poet to praise a dictator, but even in democracy a poet or writer should be cautious and not let him- or herself be dragged into the political scene, where short-term aims of power and material avarice dominate.

On the other hand, the scholarly trend, revealed in T.S. Eliot's poetry, has produced many followers who excel in extracting the motives and the images of their work from preceding art and literature. They can be witty, and often they are skilful and astute in elaborating their language. Often they rely on irony.

I doubt that wittiness, skill, astuteness, and irony can be the exclusive means for creating poetry that would endure beyond entertaining selected minds of the same fashionable guild. When poetry drifts away from the senses and immediate personal experience of reality, it becomes dry or abstract, it loses its symbiotic basis, the one revealed in the greatest literature of all times. The feeling of the other, knowing him/her/it in a deeper way than merely by mind, reason, or intellect, becomes obstructed in such a creation. One must think and feel reality not only by one's mind, but, as Unamuno wished, also through senses, blood, heart, soul, and sex. It is the greatest challenge for all literature and arts, and for philosophy.

* * *

I conclude this letter with another brief meditation about how a natural language sometimes can reflect if not predict philosophical approaches to reality. As I tried to show in my previous missive, concurring with one of the main conclusions of your *Essays*, perception of the world is unthinkable beyond the senses. Philosophy that ignores the senses lacks a fundament. Its ideas are in the air, they are weightless. They do not represent humanity, but only one part of the anatomy, the brain. Such philosophy does not represent or reflect existence, as such, but only the tiny fragment of human activity intent on gaining one's "daily bread." It is unable to answer the basic question: What is the meaning of life? What is the meaning of our activity beyond following the instinct of reason and trying to improve the earthly and material conditions of life? Does it bring us nearer to love and care for the other?

In Estonian, the word for "sense" is *meel*. Its derivates are *meeldima* (to be likeable; *sa meeldid mulle* means "I like you"), *meeldiv*, *meelepärane* (pleasant), *meelsasti* (gladly, with pleasure), *meelitama* (to flatter), *meeleline* (sensual), *meelas* (lascivous), *heameel* (joy, pleasure), *meelevaldne* (arbitrary). However, in a number of contexts *meel* overlaps completely with "reason" or "mind." *Meelehaigus* means the same as *vaimuhaigus* (mental illness), *terve meel* means "sound mind," *meeletu* is "mad," "out of reason," *meelemärkuseta* is "senseless," "without conscience."

The implication is that madness does not result from following our senses, the source of feelings and passions (and our soul and love), but the main madness of humans has been the effort (in the past and in the present) to separate reason from senses and feeling, to establish mind's superiority over all other natural faculties. Such separation is the surest way to nowhere or nothingness.

Annex 3

D.H. Lawrence: *The Rainbow* (1915)

DAVID HERBERT LAWRENCE, WHO ABANDONED this world at the age of forty-four, managed to leave to posterity thirteen novels, collections of short prose, about a hundred poems, plus plays and essays. In his puritan homeland he faced enmity. His fate was not as sad as that of Oscar Wilde, who was thrown into prison for his supposed immorality. Yet Lawrence too was taken to court several times for what was allegedly obscene in his work. His most scandalous novel, *Lady Chatterley's Lover*, which he privately published in 1928 in Florence, appeared in England in its full form only thirty years after the writer's death, having before that occasioned a lawsuit in which the accused was the publishing house Penguin.

Of well-known English writers, only E.M. Forster and Aldous Huxley paid homage to Lawrence after his passing away.

Quite a few postmodern theoreticians have claimed that modernist literature created between the two world wars was too elitist. The superficiality of such a claim is well proved by D.H. Lawrence's novels which, in contrast to novels by James Joyce, Marcel Proust, Virginia Woolf, and William Faulkner are quite easily readable: The narrative expands in them continuously from beginning to end. In that respect there are certainly similarities between Lawrence and our major Estonian novelist Anton Hansen Tammsaare. From the exclusive point of view of narrative form, neither Lawrence nor Tammsaare were modernists.

The matter is further complicated by the fact that since Cervantes' *Don Quixote* no strict division between clear-cut realism and avant-gardism has held. Despite applying a completely realistic narrative form, Lawrence introduced in literature such a strong new philosophical aspect that his novels could not be identified with 19th-century narrative fiction. His novels did not fit into the pattern of naturalism which in the work of Émile Zola and his numerous followers, since the last part of the 19th century, had become synonymous with "experimental literature."

Criticism has had similar trouble in trying to define the work of the American poet Walt Whitman, who in the mid-19th century expounded in his poems a novel love philosophy, claiming with an astonishing boldness that spiritual love without bodily love did not exist at all. For Lawrence, Whitman was a primary spiritual support and inspiration. Following the example of the American poet, Lawrence started to write poetry in free verse.

How, then, should we classify Lawrence and Whitman? Pantheism would sound old-fashioned or, in the best case, romantic. Natural philosophy is a medieval term. Naturalism indeed shows man and society as depending on biological factors, but it does so in such a fatal way that no room for anything nobler in life is left.

In Lawrence's *The Rainbow* a different feeling comes from "outside"—as mediated first by the Polish noblewoman Lydia Lensky, then by her daughter Anna, and finally by Anna's daughter Ursula. In Lydia and Anna it is an interior revolt, as it was in Virginia Woolf's characters: Gradually they adapt to the exterior set of rules of their existence.

By contrast, Ursula is a young emancipated woman who rejects marriage and vows loyalty to the rainbow that tirelessly rises over the earth. "Rainbow" becomes a symbol of woman's historical liberation. Quite surely we should not confine feminism exclusively to writing created by women. Lawrence was a modernist without formal games, a valiant spokesman of a philosophy embracing life's totality, one of the founders of the feminist novel.

One should look perhaps beyond English-language culture to find a proper way to characterize Lawrence's work. A fitting term would be "tellurism," a notion until recently applied in Spanish and Portuguese. Tellurism means intimacy in one's relation with the earth, admitting passions that have their origin in our body and blood, in sex. However, tellurism embraces something more, a germ that becomes sublimated into man's and woman's psyche from a thirst for each other in love, in a permanent revolt against a final peace. The authenticity of such love does not depend on theories.

LETTER 5

NOW AS I RETURN TO the question of knowing or, rather, feeling the "other," which seems to be a key topic in cultural studies of our times, I claim in the first place that the basis of "self"—the subject, and the opposite of the "other"—has been established in Western history almost exclusively by males. Since the most ancient times, of which we have only vague knowledge, men, physically stronger than women, have imagined themselves the superior gender. More important than the supposed—but not at all certain—bodily superiority of men has been the tendency of men to imagine themselves superior to women also in their capacity for reasoning, historically the very core of the concept of "self."

Although we know that women in some periods of ancient history were active as priests and had considerable say in social and political issues, it remains a fact that in Western Christian history, since the classical Greco-Roman era, men turned the written word and knowledge into their firm possession. The classical heritage was further fortified under German influence during the European Middle Age. All the main branches of socio-economic activity went into the hands of men. They dominated theology (the supreme science in the Middle Age), law, politics, and business, to say nothing of war-waging, which was the principal "sport" and passion of European men, something in which they hardly differed from males' basic instinct in other parts of the world.

Maybe even more than in the field of Christian theology—which had in its beginnings the vague philosophy of forgiveness and love—men sought to prove the superiority of their mental faculties, as compared with women, in wars. Military success depended greatly on mental capacity, inventing and fabricating arms, scheming astute and clever strategies, applying all kinds of corruption and fraud, which in peace-time still had at least some restrictions.

Also, in the most recent human history, in a number of areas, science has had its most rapid development in the military field. Superpowers have their secret military laboratories and industries, where mass destruction arms have been invented and produced. Though it sounds like a grotesque, maybe the greatest "achievement" of modern science is that it has invented munitions by which life on the earth can be destroyed in few hours or days. Some outstanding scientists, such as the Russian Andrei Sakharov, considered to be one of the inventors of the hydrogen bomb, as if regretting his contribution to the might of the communist superpower, became in his later years an activist for human rights, a moral man. Before him, the same can be said of Alfred Nobel, the Swedish scientist who became wealthy working in arms production. The fact that the world prizes bearing his name are not meant exclusively for scientists, but by Nobel's will one of them goes to a writer, shows that Alfred Nobel understood science's deficiency, when deprived of cultural context and made a sheer tool in the hands of power.

Shortly after your lifetime, your fellow-countryman Blaise Pascal, a major talent in mathematical and physical sciences, underwent a radical turn of conscience and abandoned sciences, becoming a religious man and a devoted Christian. The cases of Sakharov, Nobel, and Pascal, however, constitute in the general context of science an exception, rather than a rule.

* * *

Let me now return to the field of literature, in which the presence of the human "other," woman, has been much more visible than in the military domain.

Even though the field of European letters since the Middle Ages—the clumsy term the Western historians have invented to designate the lapse of at least ten centuries following the fall of the Roman Empire—has been dominated by males, woman entered the scene of literary creation almost from its very beginnings. Social conditions hardly favoured her presence as a subject and creator of literature, but there were some brave exceptions. In the vast complex of the novels and shorter narratives of chivalry, flourishing since the 12th century above all in France and Germany, there is at least one outstanding woman writer, Marie de France. She has not left us larger verse narratives, called *romans* (in English adaptation, "novels") but she wrote some shorter stories in verse in which she excelled, especially in the lyrical vein. Thus the original verse novel about the unhappy love story of Tristan and Isolde, created by some male writers, has not reached our days, but Marie de France's beautiful verse story "Chevrefoil" sums up in a few pages its main content, while adding shades to the tragic story from the point of view of the female character, Isolde.

The story is about love's magical omnipotence, its capacity to ennoble human souls and make lovers yearn for each other despite enormous distances that separate them and obstacles making the fulfillment of their desires impossible. As if symbolically, the title of Marie de France's story does not name the couple of lovers but the name of a tree. More than in most chivalrous stories told by men, Marie de France, a female creator, is open to nature. She shows nature's magic and miracles at work in love in both men and women.

At one place in your essays ("In Some Lines of Virgil," CE 980) you suppose that ideal love has been more or less an invention of men. Indeed, starting from the cult of the Virgin Mary, men have strongly contributed to the idea of pure or ideal love. However, Marie de France, in my opinion, shows that noble feelings, such as loyalty in love, once a person falls in love, transcends the merely sexual and biological call and forms a miraculous unity of spiritual and bodily features, not at all less present, but maybe even more constant in women than men.

The longer stories of chivalry, called novels, were predominantly told from the point of view of men as the authors of these stories. It is clear that nature urges men in their quest of love. However, numerous hurdles obstructing their way to the lady of their heart were just meant for trying their loyalty, to make them reveal their capacity to overcome the purely sexual instinct and enter in the field of moral values. Knights thus underwent a purification process. They became men capable of transcending their "ego," their "self" and caring for the "other."

The "knight" is *chevalier, caballero, Ritter*, a horseman who dominates the horse and is elevated over the level of simple earth, or the biological-sexual. He does not abandon it at all, as he is supported by an animal with its four legs firmly trotting the earth. Nonetheless, the knight, thus purified in a number of trials, becomes a defender of the "other," above all of virgins and defenseless ladies, against all kinds of malevolent giants and monsters embodying the predominant sexual instinct combined with rational scheming, in power structures established and dominated by males.

You mention that you hardly ever cared about novels of chivalry ("On Books," CE 560), referring to those later novels written and published mainly during the first half of the 16th century. There, indeed, stereotyped patterns emerged, extremely similar to those which flourish in our time and are meant for entertaining a large reading public. The great Spaniard Miguel de Cervantes, who wrote his first novels and plays at the time when your life came to its final stage, managed to complete, when he was over sixty, a bulky novel in two volumes, *Don Quixote*. It was initially planned as a parody of the stereotyped narratives of chivalry, but Cervantes turned it into the first European philosophical novel in prose.

To make stand forth love's magic and spiritual power, as the source of man's transcending his "self" and reaching the "other," Cervantes relied on some images never conceived in European literature before him. He introduced as the main character a madman, Don Quixote (as such, himself an "other," or more exactly, somebody oscillating between "self" and "other"). In parallel, Cervantes turned the main female character "invisible," as Don Quixote, though following his call of love and dedicating all his action and imagined heroic deeds to her, never meets her until his death.

Even though on the whole the literature of chivalry contained a lot of frivolous superficiality, and a good part of it became starting from Romanticism the main source for European fairy tales meant in the first place for children, it nonetheless formed a new type of culture in which woman stood forth with a vigour unseen in the preceding European history. I would call it the initial stage of the "other's" revolt against male dominance in European culture. It changed importantly Europe's sensibility, introducing nature and love as forces opposing the merely material-biological (symbolized by wars waged by males) and the rational (dogmatized Christian ideology as well as man's rational capacity submitted to commerce and material greed).

What I have said in the previous passages concerns the mainstream of European literature. For long centuries, creators of literature were males. Before the work of chivalrous poets and singers, telling and chanting long stories was the exclusive activity of men. Often they belonged to the courts of the early Christian rulers and had as their task to perpetuate knowledge about the great deeds of rulers, their kin and ancestors. Also, from the earliest times it was understood in the courts that these stories had much more chance to survive if they were told by poets, those capable of translating events into poetic images and expanding them by their fancy. Only such stories could enter the memory of a larger collective body (of predominantly illiterate common people) and become myths. Great deeds were identical with military victories, so the main characters of all these songs were men. The names of the original composers of these epic songs have mostly remained in the dark of ancient times, but it is obvious that often they were outstandingly talented creators.

I do not know if you ever read *Chanson de Roland*, because its print publication is not earlier than the start of the 19th century. It is a great work that has exercised deep influence on later European literature. I have always admired how the author has managed to introduce psychological features in his characters. As a rule, psychology emerges in literature in which women are involved. In *Chanson de Roland* no women appear in the action. Unlike Don Quixote, the protagonist of Cervantes's later work, Count Roland hardly has time to remember his sweetheart amid fierce battles against Saracens. All his thoughts are with his Christian king, Charlemagne, whom he would like to serve well by killing the enemies of Christianity.

The psychological features in the characters, strongly contributing to the elevated poetic tonality of the work, have to do with the fact that the creator of the work, perhaps in the middle of the 11th century, is supposed to have been a religious man, probably a monk. Clergymen whose hearts had been sweetened by the ideas of Christian piety, in which the Virgin Mary had a substantial part, had more sensibility and openness to the complexity of human soul than singers who were in the official service of the rulers, complementing the work of the early chroniclers.

* * *

In this background of men's overwhelming authority not only in governing societies and waging wars, but also in poetry, I will now deviate from the mainstream of early European literature, to tell you something that may surprise you. I will claim that in some parts of the European dark periphery the relationship between "self" and "other," at least in poetry, could have been radically different. Thus my country Estonia, though its tradition of "cultured" literature hardly goes back beyond the 19th century, has a huge treasury of traditional folksongs, collected and written down during the 19th century, but created and perpetuated orally at least since the times *Chanson de Roland* was written, if not earlier.

All the characteristic features of Estonian folksongs prove that their main creators and perpetuators were Estonian women. They are mostly presented from a woman's point of view. Thus one of the main motifs of these songs is a young woman's revenge on a man who has raped or humiliated her.

Maybe to an even greater extent than Estonian folksongs, Latvian and Lithuanian folksongs, also from the dark of the European East-Baltic periphery, reveal lyrical sensibility. Partly influenced by the German romantic era, Estonians have kept alive their tradition of folksongs. Since the Estonian national "awakening" in the middle of the 19th century, all-nation song-festivals have been held until the present time, assembling choirs from all parts of the country. They sing together traditional folksongs as well as their newer adaptations. The main force behind these festivals has always been our women and children (as choir singing is still a part of our schools' curricula).

Also, the first great work of Estonian literature, *Kalevipoeg*, an epic in twenty songs, written by Friedrich Reinhold Kreutzwald, "the Father of the Song," as he is now known, follows in the vein and spirit of traditional folksongs. It was published for the first time in 1861 in the proceedings of Gelehrte Estnische Gesellschaft—thus under scientific-academic camouflage—as a collection of genuine folksongs. As science was veneered in the tsarist empire, to which Estonia belonged, giving the work a scientific appearance was the only chance to have the epic published. It was thoroughly patriotic, passionately opposing foreign (mainly German) invaders and landlords who had turned the autochthonous population for long centuries into their peasant serfs. Thus the voice of the humiliated social and ethnic "other" emerged as camouflaged in the language of science, acceptable for the autocratic regime and its censorship.

However, first and foremost I would like to accentuate the presence in *Kalevipoeg* of the gendered "other," woman. Kreutzwald, a medical doctor and himself the son of former serfs, combined philosophical sensibility and poetic skills to create a symbiotic work, in which male and female features supported each other. The hero Kalevipoeg, a giant in his physical stature, capable of defending his country against foreign invaders, is at the same time provided with deep sensibility. His love for his mother, Linda, is one of the leitmotifs of the epic.

Though Kalevipoeg in his young days commits several grave sins, he gradually learns from his faults and becomes wiser. His is a singer and a poet, closely bound to nature. In his action he is haunted by guilt for having caused the death of a humble maid, with whom he had sexual intercourse in the initial part of the epic.

He leads the building of a capital city, Lindanisa (literarily: Linda's Breast), named in honour of his raped mother, and meant to provide shelter for women, children, the weak, and the humble. Even more important, though Kreutzwald presents the story as an epic, from the hero's birth until his death and resurrection (parallels with Christ), he relies on the traditional folksong metrics and poetic devices, such as abundant parallelisms and refrains. The narrative thus does not develop in the rhythm of straightforward progress, but is constantly slowed down, immersed in nature and lyrical images.

When Estonian "cultured" literature started to emerge at the start of the 20th century, some of its leading figures, under the influence of positivism (philosophy imitating the principles of natural sciences, in fashion in your homeland, England, and other bigger nations in those times), accused Kreutzwald of not relying in his work on "genuine" folklore and blamed him for being "scientifically incorrect."

One may ask: What poetic work *is* scientifically correct? Today, *Kalevipoeg* has become a major mythical and folkloric work. Its motifs penetrate all subsequent Estonian culture. One of the accusations by our early men of letters against Kreutzwald was that he did not follow faithfully the epic pattern as such, with its dominating masculine features. I would ask in my turn: What gods have established the rule that epic works should carry masculine features and exclude feminine sensibility? I would rather see in our "peripheral" Kreutzwald a great introducer of the feminine consciousness into the epical tradition, a creator of a symbiotic work, representing human being (in Estonian: *inimene*, that does not mean "man" nor "woman") in such a way that male and female consciousness enters in a mutually enriching relationship.

I am glad to say that I am not alone in my assertions of *Kalevipoeg*'s novelty and excellence as an epic. Kreutzwald's chef-d'oeuvre has been translated fully into a dozen foreign languages. At the start of our second millennium, its translation in your mother language was published by one of the most prestigious Parisian publishing houses, while a second English translation as well as a translation into the Hindi language has recently been published.

* * *

But I am far from idealizing the presence of the gendered "other" in my native Estonia, as a whole. It may be because of our sad historical background, of being forced into humiliating slavery by bigger nations, that democratic habits in my country do not have deeper roots. In comparison with Scandinavian countries, geographically close to us, we have lagged far behind in developing gender balance. Our Estonian state, as a political unit between the two world wars, was entirely male-made. The Soviet-Russian socialist system, to which our country was annexed for nearly half a century, officially proclaimed gender equality, but in practice it was dominated by males. I remember from my past that only the minister of culture of the Soviet Union (as well as Soviet Estonia) was a woman; all the rest of the political (and military) leaders were men.

Such an extreme lack of gender balance also taints my present-day Estonia. Women may sing at our song festivals; they are admitted to our ritual military forces; they act also as church pastors; they form the main body of our schoolteachers and librarians; they are active as medical doctors. But all the principal tools of political-economical power are moved my males who also, correspondingly, accumulate in their pockets the bulk of the material wealth produced by the nation.

One has to admit that democratic processes, gradually leading to changes in gender relations in Europe, have developed basically in European centres, France being one of the main nations in the vanguard of these changes.

Annex 4

Gustave Flaubert: *Sentimental Education* (1869)

THE RUSSIAN PHILOSOPHER OF LITERATURE Mikhail Bakhtin, when researching the poetics of the novels by Fyodor Dostoyevsky, set forth the notion of polyphony. Polyphony is also the principal novelty in Gustave Flaubert's *Sentimental Education*. The teacher of both Dostoyevsky and Flaubert was the "arch-polyphonist" Miguel de Cervantes.

In 1971/1972 the philosopher and writer Jean-Paul Sartre published a three-volume essay *The Family Idiot: Gustave Flaubert (1821–1857)* in which he made an attempt to revalue Flaubert's work and ideas from the Marxist-existentialist point of view. It was a great enterprise, which nonetheless did not bear mellow fruit, just because Flaubert's work was approached from a single and definite point of view.

There has been a lot of discussion about Flaubert. Between the pages of my home copy of the Estonian translation of *L'Éducation sentimentale* I found an offprint of an article published in our literary journal *Looming*, with a dedication: "To Jüri Talvet, from author, in Pärnu, 1.I 1981." The author was Albert Trummal, a late colleague, whose doctoral thesis and most of his mature work had Flaubert as its focus. An extensive introductory essay for the above-mentioned translation was written by Ott Ojamaa, one of our leading connoisseurs of French literature, a long-time colleague of Trummal. It is not difficult to see that Ojamaa too had Flaubert very close to his heart. He quotes a marginal note written about Flaubert in the time of WWI by Friedebert Tuglas, a prominent Estonian intellectual and writer of the first half of the 20th century. Tuglas saw in Flaubert an ideal—a "mind-smith," a disciple of genuine art who despite "bustling in the mind's market" continued his mission, "equally hating the petty-bourgeois and that proud, but vain and superficial soul whom he called 'artist.'"

Now as we read *Sentimental Education*, supposedly one of Flaubert's most autobiographical works, how else could we define the main character Frédéric Moreau except as a dilettante artist's soul who would never become a genuine artist, and his beloved Madame Arnaux as a petty bourgeois, surrendered to her fate, devoted to her home and children despite the fact that her husband cheats on her with his mistresses?

Something in the scheme of young Tuglas would not work. His criticism of our epic *Kalevipoeg*, created by F.R. Kreutzwald, did not work either. Flaubert and Kreutzwald are writers—in fact, contemporaries, both *Kalevipoeg* and *L'Éducation sentimentale* having been written in the 1860s—whose work would transcend Tuglas' basically rationalistic point of view.

Cervantes could help us to come nearer to Flaubert. In *Don Quixote* he made "the invisible Dulcinea"—a woman who never appears bodily on the pages of the voluminous novel—direct and coordinate all the action. In *Sentimental Education* we see how Frédéric already on page 4 falls in love with a lady of Spanish complexion, Madame Arnaux. She however remains for a long time for Frédéric as unattainable as Dulcinea was for Don Quixote. Only in the middle of the novel's action does Frédéric, with the reader of the novel, find out for the first time that Madame Arnaux is nonetheless not indifferent towards him. Till the end of the novel Frédéric—though being thoroughly earthy and sensual, a man predisposed to enjoy life, no matter if he is bourgeois or noble—does not have sexual contact with Madame Arnaux.

Yet Flaubert shows how much Frédéric desires Madame Arnaux: There are long descriptions of how Frédéric seeks to meet his beloved and tries to find ways how to get into contact with her. Quest constitutes the marrow of the novel, just as the utmost goal of Don Quixote's adventure was love. Love makes absurd all theories about social classes—despite dogmatic sociology and attempts like those of Sartre to engraft Marxism onto existentialism.

A Marxist-sociologist would attack Madame Arnaux for her indulgent passivity. But let us notice: Woman's "unmovable" love makes the whole novel move, it forces man to open himself and reveal his deeper contradictions and weaknesses, his vulgarity and, still, somewhere in the inner depth something that does not yield to the daily routine of earthiness.

Ott Ojamaa explains quite pointedly in his introductory essay that French "sentiment" does not mean a transitory emotion, but derives rather from what would have its equivalent in the Estonian *tundmine*. In the terms of Miguel de Unamuno it would be the "sense of life." Flaubert turns the clarification of "sense of life" into his novel's axis. The entire society with its ideological mess, passions, ideas, vanities and ambitions is made to turn around it. There are as many voices as people. In a way, *Sentimental Education* is a novel of the absurd. As ever, the source of the absurd is the attempt to subdue life's polyphony to a single voice, a single instinct—reason.

LETTER 6

"Peripheries" cannot do without "centres," women cannot do without men, soul and spirit cannot do without reason, and vice versa. The task is to change the balance in their mutual relations, which until recently have been strongly and violently biased in favour of "centres," men, and reason. When women scholars and activists today speak of the achievements and victories of their gender in the historical gender battles, they seldom credit the men of letters and singers, troubadours and *Minnesingers*, who forged chivalrous culture, moving noblewomen into the centre of men's attention and action, and thus facilitating the process of woman's liberation.

Also your age, the Renaissance, widened importantly the circle of awakened women, especially as the crucial technical innovation, book-printing, accelerated literacy beyond the circles of nobility. Women as creators of significant literature were still rare, but they were among the most avid readers of literary works. Men, creators of literature, could not ignore the growing reading public beyond their own gender. The English translator of your *Complete Essays*, M.A. Screech, mentions in his introduction to the book that French noblewomen highly appreciated Raymond Sebond's *Theologia naturalis* long before you, following the will and wish of your father, undertook its translation (some 1000 pages) into French. Screech hints at the possibility that Princess Marguerite, the later queen Marguerite de Navarre, herself an outstanding liberal-minded writer, asked you to write an essay about Sebond's work.

I do not know if you ever read any poems by Louise Labé. In the later literary histories she hardly occupies such an outstanding position in French or European Renaissance letters as do your favourites Pierre de Ronsard or Joachim De Bellay. Yet the fact itself that she came from the middle class (she was the daughter of a rope-maker) is significant. Besides, her poems, though few in number, transcend the idealized pattern of Renaissance lyric poetry, established by Petrarch and faithfully followed and expanded throughout the work of most men who in the 16th century wrote sonnets, eclogues, or chansons.

Since the earliest days of the Renaissance in Italy, the sensible line in culture, open to the other gender, was taken up by those learned men who were not directly linked with the Church, which was suspicious of nature and natural love between humans. As those learned men tried to revive the cultural heritage of ancient Greece and Rome, and were inspired in their work by it, they came to be called humanists (those dealing with human science, rather than with heavenly science, or theology). I do not know if you, Montaigne, ever accepted the label of "humanist," but by all criteria of humanism, as an historical phenomenon, you certainly were among the most eminent humanist writers of your time. Anyone who reads your *Essays* will immediately notice your great indebtedness to the ancient thinkers and writers whose work you mention and quote often in expanding your own thoughts.

In my days there is a lot of confusion about the phenomenon of humanism. Some postmodern theorists have tried to identify it with the work of rationally inclined scholars. I find their intuition incorrect. Scholarly commentators on ancient culture, those working under the spell of the "rationality" of such ancient philosophers as Aristotle and Plato, were heirs of male-formed reason and rationality, but as far as I can judge from my reading of the work of Erasmus, Rabelais, and yourself, you did not follow that line at all, but on the contrary, you and the other best-known humanist writers worked in constant opposition to scholarly-rational knowledge which was inclined to produce dogmatic preaching and to propound truths severed from nature and life's totality.

* * *

The *opus magnum* of Dante Alighieri, the great Italian who made a huge "leap" from the Middle Ages to new Renaissance consciousness, based on the individual, is filled with dogmatic-rational schemes and symbols. In his *Commedia* (or *Divina Commedia*, as the long philosophic poem came to be titled), Dante depicted through a series of poetic-symbolic images his own soul's journey in the otherworld, from sin to God (whose gender he did not determine directly, but revealed in a symbiosis of love (*amore*, masculine gender) and light (*luce*, feminine)). Similarly, in the guiding of his symbolic journey, Dante combines the masculine and the feminine. The Roman poet Virgil, whom you, too, highly revered, is shown in *Divina Commedia* as symbolizing human reason. But that faculty alone is not sufficient to reach God. Dante's supreme guide to God is Beatrice, a noblewoman with whom Dante in his life fell in love. Thus the gender-contradiction becomes mitigated. Beatrice resembles the Virgin Mary, the mediator between human and heavenly love.

The fact that Dante in his philosophic essay *Convivio* imagined Ethics as standing higher than Metaphysics is also significant. Ethics by its very essence is a faculty that shows "self's" openness to the "other," the need of the "self" in its behaviour to take into account the existence of the "other." Metaphysics, on the contrary, can perfectly be subject-derived and, in fact, in the history of ideas it has been a province of male reasoning.

Dante Alighieri did not consciously research ancient philosophers' or writers' work, but he intuitively grasped some of Plato's ideas from the work of his immediate predecessors, the Italian poets who established *dolce stil nuovo*, praising pure divine love as an ideal, and making it superior to love as natural passion. The greatest lyric poet of 14th-century Italy, Francesco Petrarch, followed the same line, but stayed closer to nature. His love for Laura, as reflected in his collection of lyric poems, *Canzoniere*, is often defined as platonic. However, a closer look at these poems would reveal Petrarch's hidden sexual passion. He conceived love as embracing both soul and body, an urge both divine and earthly, in their never stable or steady interaction.

Petrarch's friend and fellow-writer Giovanni Boccaccio appears to posterity as a thoroughly earthy man, the author of the *Decameron* (which, as you say, Montaigne, you enjoyed), a collection of stories telling mainly about human passions and vices, showing love "in practice," not elevated above coarse material factors. Whatever the moral of his particular stories, Boccaccio is a radically pioneering European writer who emphasized nature and natural love as the main driving force, hidden or open, of all human activity. As for the gendered "other," Boccaccio was the first European writer to give woman her own voice. Far more extensively than any other writer, Boccaccio let women speak, express an interior self. Even though it was woman as imagined by a man, her entering the scene with agency began to undermine the dominance of the masculine "self," the embodiment of male reasoning.

A reader of the *Decameron* might not notice one structural detail, but it is important. In the frame story, women outnumber men, seven to three. One cannot claim that Boccaccio let young men speak of coarse bodily pleasures and eroticism, leaving only virtuous and noble action (by the way, not at all missing in *Decameron*) for young ladies, as their share in story-telling. Female narrators are a clear majority, and the *Decameron* overwhelmingly shows humans' natural passions in action: Boccaccio, by this symbolic-formal narrative device, hints at womankind's intimate relation to the natural and biological-sexual core of existence, that which has been neutralized, deformed, and violated by man's historical action.

Also, in a more direct sense of giving woman her voice, Boccaccio significantly widens the role of speech in his stories. Especially his larger stories are not at all told directly by the narrator (Boccaccio). The author often relies on mediating narrators. The characters, including a great number of women, are shown as having their individual voice and philosophy. Even before the *Decameron*, Boccaccio wrote his short novel *Fiammetta*, a most admirable achievement in presenting the narrated reality—including the intimately amorous—from the point of view of woman. At the same time one should not forget that Boccaccio was a great admirer of Dante Alighieri's work and, in fact, the first commentator on Dante's *Commedia*. Virtue and noble spirit in women, especially in young women, capable by their love of purifying and ennobling men, was a theme of Boccaccio's (as can be seen from his beautiful lyrical-mythical short novel in verse *Ninfale fiesolano* and the prose story of his young days, *Ameto*).

The next landmark in making the voice of the gendered other heard in European literature was *Celestina*, or *Tragicomedy of Calisto and Melibea*, attributed to a descendent of converted Spanish Jews, Fernando de Rojas. Its earliest version dates from the year 1499, shortly after the discovery and the conquest by Spaniards and Portuguese of the New World had begun. The gendered "other" in this work has its very special complement, as it simultaneously represents the social "other," thus strongly contrasting the corpus of chivalrous literature. The main spokeswoman of this hybrid work, combining the features of both a prose novel and a play, is an old bawd called Celestina. The name (from the Latin *caelestis*—'heavenly'; maybe also an allusion to Pope Celestine V, the founder of the religious order of Celestines) is ironical: Celestina helps young people to taste earthly lovemaking, which they surely did not enjoy less than celestial love of God promised by the Church to pure souls in the afterworld.

Although it is initially a love story of two young people, Calisto and Melibea, who for some reason (maybe for their social differences) cannot meet in public, soon Celestina emerges as the protagonist. In her long monologues she justifies earthly love as the very foundation of all life, human life no less than that of the rest of nature, which humans are part of by God's own will. In Celestina's philosophy, God is the creator of the world, and all that is created by God is good. The work, however, has an unhappy end. Celestina is killed by Calisto's greedy servants, Calisto dies in an accident, and Melibea, after expounding her unhappy story in a monologue, commits suicide. The work could be seen as a warning about the sad consequences of earthly love, but it is definitely more than that, since the source of the evil is human scheming (social conventions imposed by male reasoning) against natural love (earthly and celestial) as the work of God.

* * *

In your essays you make only indirect references to the work of Erasmus of Rotterdam, the great Dutchman who together with his friend, the Englishman Thomas More, have come in later centuries to embody the initial glory of European humanism. Erasmus was among the most learned men in the Europe of his time and, as such, was respected by princes and popes, but his philosophy, like yours, was based on respecting life's totality. Like you, Erasmus attacked and ridiculed bookish philosophers, scholastics, and pedants who developed their knowledge by pure rational speculations, driving reason away from its natural basis. Like you, especially in the mature part of your essays, he criticized the Stoics for their effort to make reason self-sufficient and to deny human feelings and passions.

I do not think Erasmus was successful in developing his philosophy into a coherent system, but why should we consider a rationally constructed systematic philosophy (of which we have one of the most perfect examples in the idealistic work of the German Georg Wilhelm Friedrich Hegel, at the start of the 19th century) superior to a philosophy that is in process, unfinished, but already including some essential ideas about the meaning of our existence?

In my opinion Erasmus' ideas appear in their most spontaneous brilliance in his small book, *The Praise of Folly*. It is a prose satire employing images that one usually finds in belletristic works, not in philosophical treatises. Erasmus demonstrates wonderfully how philosophy and literary image are compatible, forming a symbiosis not at all inferior to those works in which philosophy is run into the ditch of pure reasoning.

The advantage of an image over an idea (despite their shared origin, as both refer to visually perceived form) is that the former is made of the senses and for the senses or, rather, unites thought with the senses in such a way that they represent more than merely human mind and its ratiocinations. They reflect wisdom emanating from the totality of existence, in which all human faculties are equally important, and on which all converge. They represent man and woman in such a way that neither is a definite "self" or a fatal "other": The genders continuously interchange their roles and values. It is an endless dynamic symbiosis.

Like Boccaccio and Rojas before him, Erasmus expounded his philosophy by relying on a female protagonist, though in this case she is a clear-cut philosophic symbol. Erasmus presented his philosophic discourse as a monologue uttered by a woman, named Moria (Folly). Her self-praise, in part serious and in part ironical, makes the image dynamic and ambiguous. It is in a movement, unfinished.

Erasmus wittily demonstrates the same conclusions you, Montaigne, have echoed in your essays. Life's totality (represented in Erasmus' book by the woman Moria) comprises the supreme value. Love in all its embodiments is its ferment and basis. It is the will and creation of ancient gods as well as of the Christian God. Its sources are senses, passions, and feeling, those human faculties that learned and scholarly men have considered inferior to reason and mind. In contrast, folly appears in Moria's monologue as the great foundation on which the living world stands.

It is Erasmus' double irony: Moria (Folly) is not really folly, but wisdom, approved by gods, by which the world exists. By contrast, human reason, generally considered as the supreme faculty (Aristotle's "rational animal" which you, Montaigne, ridiculed in "An Apology for Raymond Semond") differentiating mankind from the rest of nature, appears as genuine folly, especially when separated from nature and violating the harmony and balance established by nature or the Supreme Creator.

In the final part of his masterpiece, continuing to combine irony with seriousness, Erasmus confesses that maybe Christianity itself is also a kind of folly …

Less ambiguously, Erasmus attacked tyrants and autocrats who violate and humiliate the "other," turning people into slaves in the name of their own welfare and pleasure. Erasmus also offered devastating criticism of militarism, the great historical male passion. He showed it as contradicting the very principles of both Christianity and nature, as it had shed destruction and death all over Europe, causing suffering and misery to millions of people.

Several of Erasmus' ideas were taken up by your countryman François Rabelais in his book *Gargantua and Pantagruel* (which, too, was among the books you liked). Like *The Praise of Folly*, Rabelais' chef-d'oeuvre is a philosophical satire. However, Rabelais employed the form of novel, in the sense that its basis is a story, not just a string of loosely connected images. The book was directly influenced by chivalrous narratives which by that time had undergone a thorough modification, becoming especially in Spain a diversion for quite a wide reading public.

Also in Italy, several influential works in the genre of extensive chivalrous narratives in verse were turned into comedies, including coarse details from everyday popular life and folkloric literature. Thus, Luigi Pulci in the second half of the 15th century introduced coarsely comical characters, a couple of giants, in his burlesque chivalrous epic *Morgante*. "High" and "low" literature started to intermingle.

Following the model of Pulci's epic, but writing instead in prose, Rabelais produced a highly fantastic work, based on grotesque exaggerations and including a long series of intentionally obscene images and details (lavish episodes describing urinating, defecating, eating, drinking, and body parts that for long Christian centuries had been taboo). Even for many of my students today, Rabelais' way of expression, which relies extensively on lexical obscenities not found in dictionaries, seems repugnant.

In my day, with its practically unlimited individual freedom, especially younger writers are fond of such vocabulary, trying to shock the reader by openly accentuated details of human intimate organs and their natural functions. Yet there is a difference. Rabelais' vocabulary articulated a bold philosophy. He relied on anatomic-naturalistic images and the language of obscenities to show nature's greatness, energy, and power emerging from beneath all human speculations, dogmatic preaching, and violation of nature by the Church in alliance with official power structures along centuries.

Rabelais was aware of the need for harmony between spirit and body, but thought it must be recreated and revived on the basis of nature. He had read the works of Erasmus and Thomas More, as well as those of ancient thinkers and writers. The image of "Utopia" as a state of (relative) harmony, provided by Thomas More in his small witty book *Utopia* (not at all devoid of irony and ambiguity in a number of its episodes) was very well known to Rabelais. He even called Gargantua's kingdom Utopia, thus paying a direct homage to the valiant English humanist, executed in Rabelais' lifetime by the English tyrant King Henry VIII.

Thomas More envisaged an imaginary island, Utopia (whose name itself included playful language irony: "a non-existing place"), constructed on the principles of political democracy and the abolishment of private ownership. It was a landmark "leap" of imagination into future centuries. Starting from the end of the 18th century, a series of revolutions shook Europe. An ever growing political-economical power centre was formed in North America, called the United States.

While revolutions in the 19th century had as their main aim abolishing the privileges of the hereditary nobility, the 1917 revolution shaking the Russian tsarist empire caused the emergence of a totally new socio-economic system, similar to the one envisaged in More's *Utopia* and in the works of some utopian dreamers along the 18th and 19th centuries. The new socio-economic organization of life, denying private ownership and based on the principles of collectivism, now in its more moderate, now more radical version, came to be called socialism or communism. It naturally meant a huge "leap" in changing the relations between "self" and "other," socially and in the gendered sense.

Efforts to put More's Utopia into practice, at least for the time being, have failed. Yet in the course of these (often tragic) developments, the world has been significantly divided into three types of societies. After WWII, the rich Western countries were imagined as the "first world," the so called socialist countries (which indeed managed to liquidate elementary or extreme poverty) were imagined (more than being directly called) as the "second world," while the largest part of poor and economically underdeveloped countries became to be called the "third world."

At the start of the 21st century, the last of three terms is still widely in circulation, as poverty has remained and has even increased in the bigger part of the world. The "first world" continues to subdivide (as shown by the annual meetings of the leaders of the world's eight or twenty largest economies), while the majority of former socialist countries, including the former communist superpowers Russia and China, have introduced since the early 1990s principles of capitalist market economics, in an attempt to catch up with the "first world" and share in its material welfare.

Annex 5

Virginia Woolf: *Mrs. Dalloway* (1925)

VIRGINIA WOOLF ENTERED THE WIDER Estonian consciousness in the 1970s mysteriously, vaguely, as a hint disturbing by its obscurity, without her earthly body (which she had banished from this world early in WWII), even without her spiritual body (because her work had not yet been translated into Estonian). The first translation did not appear until 1983. She infiltrated invisibly, because Virginia Woolf is not among the characters in the play by the American writer Edward Albee (1928–2016) and no one in the work says who Virginia Woolf was or explains the meaning of the song fragment "Who's Afraid of Virginia Woolf?," intoned periodically by Martha and George, the protagonists of the absurdist and Strindberg-like matrimonial drama, loaded with psychological tension.

The play was staged successfully by Adolph Shapiro in the theatre of Pärnu in 1978 and 1979. In the main roles, Linda Rummo and Aarne Üksküla excelled with brilliance. It was an epoch when in Estonia great theatre was performed. A wide public read and experienced its meanings from what was said and what was omitted. Virginia Woolf was noticed, her name started to sing in the ears of many people. That her work had not been translated earlier showed by itself that there had to be about her something not favoured by the communist regime and its official culture.

Some ten years earlier there had been similar confusion concerning Virginia Woolf in Prague. Albee had recently written his play and was visiting the Socialist Republic of Czechoslovakia. The translator had a bold idea: He changed the title of the play to "Who's Afraid of Franz Kafka?"

Thus Edward Albee, Virginia Woolf, the Czech translator, and Franz Kafka, by their joint effort helped to build up an opposition against the totalitarian regime, in the language that Woolf and Kafka created in the initial quarter of the 20th century—to defy other, different powers. Yet there is no difference. Power is power—violence, anger, arrogance against nature and humans, against nobleness and beauty.

The fragile Englishwoman Virginia Woolf published in 1929 a longer essay, *A Room of One's Own*. The most fervent of the combat units of feminism have consecrated it as their manifesto. Woolf, however, did not simplify anything. The narrative manner of realism did not satisfy her. She was looking for forms that by themselves would create a premise for letting the "other" speak. Thus the reader of *Mrs. Dalloway* grasps at once that something is working quite differently there, as compared with an average novel. Woolf starts to narrate from the point of view of a character, touches his / her thoughts, but then quite unexpectedly assumes the point of view of another character. The "other" is turned suddenly into "self," and vice versa.

It appears that the reader cannot trust his/her own judgment or identify him- / herself with a concrete character. The characters slip out of immediate grasp; they are more complicated than sociological schemes or the human types created by Honoré de Balzac in his novels, in the mid-19th century. Even the simplest person has a unique soul; everyone is waiting for love. In her short narrative "Kew Gardens," Woolf registers people, their behaviour and psychical states through the eyes of a snail that moves from one flowerbed to another.

With Marcel Proust, James Joyce and William Faulkner, Virginia Woolf belongs, almost the only woman in a long line of males, among the leading renovators of the novel between the two world wars.

Since the "high society" of Estonia is a relatively new phenomenon, we have two separate words to designate what in several bigger languages has only one signifier: society. Woolf herself belonged to the English intellectual elite, which in history has been in the closest way intertwined with power elite, that is, with the social group that has imagined itself as society, but in fact has imposed crudely its "own" rules, overwhelmingly shaped by male reason, on the weaker part of society.

The Prime Minister's wife Mrs. Dalloway knows that she cannot escape conformity with her husband and society. Yet until the end an interior revolt persists in her. It may be hidden and suppressed, but it is the reason why the most powerful and influential part of this world's society continue to be afraid of Virginia Woolf, Franz Kafka, and Juhan Liiv, now and in the time to come.

LETTER 7

MOST GREAT REVOLUTIONS HAVE FAILED to achieve the results declared in their manifestos and programs. Still, as their "by-products," evident shifts in ideological attitudes have taken place. These have had a much longer-lasting influence than the consequences of innumerable wars waged by males in the name of merely material wealth and power. To mention an example of the most recent past of Europe, three East-Baltic nations, Estonia, Latvia, and Lithuania, with a total population scarcely reaching over six million people, but covering a considerable patch of territory on the shores of the Baltic Sea, became politically independent mainly as the result of the radical ideological turns that led to the collapse of both empires, of which they formerly were a part.

Without the revolutionary processes in the "centres" of these empires, their numerous peripheral nations, whatever the pressure from the outside, could never have won their political freedom. The socialist revolution of 1917 was the work of communist ideology pushing into movement Russia's vast proletariat and peasantry. It was possible because Russia had never had any democratic system, with its need for a well-established middle class. When the "centre" of Soviet Russia became strong enough by the end of the 1930s, it could swallow again, in the course of WWII, all three East-Baltic republics, whose political independence thus was limited to scarce twenty years.

The ideological liberalization movement, called "perestroika," triggered from inside the very "centre" by some valiant Russians, Mikhail Gorbachev and Boris Yeltsin, from the middle of the 1980s—as they looked for normalizing relations with democratic West—led to the collapse of the whole socialist empire. Estonia, Latvia, and Lithuania were the only peripheral republics of the former Soviet Union that became after these developments fully integrated to West. They joined the European Union and the Western military defense alliance, NATO, of which the mightiest unit is the army of the trans-Atlantic superpower, the U.S.

Womankind's gradual liberation has also been a kind of a "by-product" of revolutions incited mainly by males. But maybe because the process of woman's emancipation and liberation has been a "by-product," not a main goal of any of the revolutionary turns known to us, it has been less affected by concrete material instincts of males. Instead, it has shown more openness to ideas and sensibility produced by cultural process, with literary creation in its perpetual vanguard. These ideas, essentially intertwined with philosophy, have had a far deeper influence on humankind's consciousness than wars and revolutions, made in the hope of a rapid change (which never came true).

Evolution in nature has taken thousands and maybe millions of years. Why should we suppose that human revolutions could lead to immediate and rapid changes? Is humanity not a part of nature? Or, to ask it more provocatively: Is woman and childbirth not a part of nature? And why should one imagine that males, with their stronger inclination (as compared with women) to fabricate artificiality and invent techniques driven away from nature, could ever achieve by their revolutions and wars any improvement for humankind in its totality? Their victories are short-lived. Sooner or later their basic material instincts of wealth and power re-emerge, however skilful their verbal techniques in promising new paradises on the earth.

* * *

Despite the above, it is certain that a sensible minority of males, the "knights of spirit," have substantially contributed to the awakening of the gendered "other," woman, thus contributing to premises for her overcoming her status of eternal "other" and for her participation in the ideological-creative process as an independent subject, her "self." North and South of Europe established in this sense a fruitful dialogue in your lifetime and in the decades that followed, still in the wake of the Renaissance. Women were socially more liberated in Southern Europe.

For instance, when theatre became a major socio-cultural phenomenon toward the end of 16th century—when you wrote your *Essays*—with English and Spanish professional drama and theatre in its vanguard, in Tudor England women could not act on the stage. Instead, the roles of female characters were performed by men. In Spain, in contrast, actresses not only could demonstrate their talent and beauty on the theatrical stage, but by their presence itself made a much more immediate public impact than male actors, however skilfully disguised as women, could have hoped to achieve. Their evident success as "subjects" of creativity, revealing their personality as artists, might have been the weightiest factor in their centrality to the work of Spanish dramatic authors.

Thus woman's presence, especially in active and dynamic roles revealing her psychology and creative talents, is much more visible in the work of Lope de Vega, Tirso de Molina and Calderón de la Barca than in Shakespeare's dramas, to mention only some of the greatest dramatists of both countries. Shakespeare brilliantly depicted women as victims of males' power aspirations and intrigues (Ophelia in *Hamlet*, Desdemona in *Othello*, as the brightest examples). He aroused compassion and pity, as the first great English writer Geoffrey Chaucer did in several of his *Canterbury Tales*. Both Chaucer and Shakespeare were greatly indebted to Southern-European writers, Boccaccio and Petrarch.

At the same time Shakespeare did not idealize women. On the contrary, he showed that in the greed of power and rational intriguing women not only could equal men, but be even more steady and ruthless (Lady Macbeth, in *Macbeth*, the elder daughters of Lear, in *King Lear*). More than any other dramatist, Shakespeare penetrated into the dark realm of the evil in the psyche of both men and women.

In the psychological aspect the leading Spanish playwrights were less capable than Shakespeare. They hardly managed to create such great characters as Hamlet, King Lear, Macbeth, Lady Macbeth, Othello, Romeo, Juliet, Shylock, Iago, Falstaff, and others who have become, especially since the Romantic Period, widely known in the world's cultural scene. But it would be wrong to conclude that Spanish "Golden Age" plays have had less international influence because they lack characters based on such psychological contradiction or ambiguity. The issue instead is a "technical" difficulty, namely that Spanish Baroque drama employs a variety of verse and rhyme patterns not easily translatable into other languages. As France started to dominate Europe's cultural scene from the second half of the 17th century, while Spain was gradually reduced to France's cultural periphery, Europe "forgot" about the old treasures of Spanish theatre for nearly two centuries. Only with the radical turn of cultural ideology in Romanticism could European "periphery" establish a renewed dialogue with "centre."

I doubt that Lope de Vega ever wrote a play without women involved in the action. Perhaps his own amorous attentions helped him to portray women with intimate nuance. Besides, Lope de Vega was a great Western pioneering dramatist in letting the social "other" enter on the stage. A whole series of his plays show peasants as protagonists, defying violence on the part of feudal landlords and military dignitaries. Plots generally focus on the attempts of feudal landlords, relying on their authority, to rape and humiliate peasant girls. The fathers and brothers of the girls are on the alert, trying to avoid by all means violation of their "honour." Once "honour," greatly coinciding with family prestige in the eyes of a community, was violated, it required revenge. Such situations, with light variations, are common to all the best-known plays of Lope de Vega. The topic continued in Calderón's drama of honour. In this context of the social and also gendered "other," woman often appeared on the stage of the Spanish "Golden Age" theatre.

In one of his best-known plays, *Fuenteovejuna*, Lope de Vega did what would have been absolutely unimaginable in the rest of

European theatre. The feudal landlord crudely violates the honour of peasant girls of a village called Fuenteovejuna. Following an act of the same kind in the drama, the village people spontaneously revolt against the landlord. Simple village women passionately take part in the revolt. In their bold defiance of humiliation, they become even more visible than men on the scene.

It is interesting that when in the 1920s the play was translated into Estonian and staged at one of the main Estonian theatres, the title of the play was changed, to make it more understandable for the Estonian public: "Women's Revolt." Even though the revolt in Lope de Vega's play is a thoroughly local incident, it reflects the start of changes of social attitudes to the "other" in the broader landscape of Western history.

* * *

Tirso de Molina is the literary pseudonym of the Spanish playwright Gabriel Téllez, a monk who at the start of the 17th century introduced in Western culture the character and myth of Don Juan. Especially since Molière in the second half of the 17th century reshaped Don Juan's story in a prose comedy, the myth has been tremendously productive. Direct repercussions or motifs of the myth and the image of Don Juan have appeared in countless works of literature and art throughout the following centuries.

There are some other great literary characters whose image has been widely circulating: Shakespeare's Hamlet, Cervantes' Don Quixote, Goethe's Faust. All are contradictory, but positive features clearly prevail: Hamlet doubts the sense of fighting against corrupted power, but the longer he doubts, the more penetrating his denouncement of power's abuses appears. Don Quixote is a madman, not bound by the norms imposed on the world of the sane. In the name of love, following the codes of medieval knights, he fights restlessly against all human and social vices which since the end of the chivalrous dream have crowded the increasingly materialistic world.

The legend of Faust, a magician who is said to have lived in Germany in the days of your youth, was first echoed in an anonymous German popular book towards the end of your century. Almost immediately after, it was taken up by the English dramatist Christopher Marlowe, who wrote a play called *The Tragical History of Dr. Faust.* However, the same legend can be found in medieval literature long before. Calderón echoed the motif in his play *El mágico prodigioso.* Towards the end of the 18th century, the German Johann Wolfgang von Goethe became attracted by the topic. He synthesized all previous sources of the legend in a majestic philosophical drama in verse, *Faust.* Contrary to what happened to Faust in the German popular book and also in Marlowe's play of your life-time (condemned for his pact with Satan, Faust's fall was inevitable, he had to go to Hell), Goethe let Faust's soul be redeemed by the Virgin Mary, taking into account that despite his initial sinning, this thoughtful man, akin to Hamlet, had overcome his individualism and wanted to devote himself to the improvement of humankind.

In this philosophical background, Don Juan may seem a light and frivolous figure. He too has positive features (he is a bold, healthy, handsome, materialistically-minded young man who does not fear God's punishment and is not afraid of the Devil), but his main action is a series of love-making adventures, in which his victims are young women whom he abandons to shame, after having robbed them of their "honour," that is, their virginity.

Tirso de Molina's original Don Juan in his *El burlador de Sevilla y convidado de piedra* has been generally forgotten, being predominantly replaced by the image forged by Molière. Yet in my opinion it is only in the original play by Tirso de Molina that Don Juan appears in his full mythical potentiality, including sexual coarseness as well as lyrical ingredients, lost in Molière's later adaptation. The original Don Juan is clearly a negative character, embodying the sexual drive in any healthy young man. His love conquests, in which he treats equally noble-ladies and humble prostitutes, leaving the former without "honour" and the latter without money, reflect symbolically the "progress" and "victories" of male kind over the "other," both in the gendered and the social respect.

However, what is equally important in the play is the young women's reaction. Leaving alone Seville's prostitutes, social outcasts deprived of any voice of their own, women humiliated by Don Juan in Tirso de Molina's original presentation not only complain of their unhappy fate, but they make their unified voice of protest, transcending social layers, heard to power, people, and God. Tirso de Molina lets emerge from his play an astonishingly powerful symbol of women's revolt against men, thus envisaging the historical process of deep changes in inter-gender relations.

It is not a utopia. It is a fully real process whose widening scope we at the start of the 21st century witness. Not only in the West, but also in oriental countries, especially in those dominated by Islam, there are signs of woman's historical awakening. It is the main hope for certain shifts in human consciousness. It is a long-term process, but it has begun.

Annex 6

Peter Høeg: *Smilla's Sense of Snow* (1992)

BY HIS WORK (WITH THE original title in Danish *Frøken Smillas for-nemmelse for sne*), Peter Høeg pursues one of the main challenges faced by the contemporary novel: the need to overcome postmodern fragmentation, to aspire to a new philosophical symbiosis.

It is by no means an easy book to read. It would be much simpler to watch the film made from it. Yet films rely on other means than literary expression. They are made above all in the language of visuality. There, in most cases, some part is lost of the freedom of imagination, born—paradoxically—only from a book's monotonous printed signs, letters.

For that reason I still recommend the reading of Peter Høeg's novel, one of the most outstanding achievements in the genre of the novel in the 1990s, the period of the slow dying-down of postmodern cultural philosophy. The battle of postmodernism against "grand narratives" had culminated in praise of the fragment, in particularism. The 1990s were the period of literature's neo-medieval generic fragmentation, incarnated by fiction about writing novels, novels about sexual minorities, action-novels, horror novels, science-fiction, etc. Everyone has a fragment of the novel genre, with its corresponding rules and technique. Just as medieval monks had among their main tasks copying ancient texts, though they seldom understood these texts, most postmodern writers have hoped to create new meanings by rewriting a generic fragment.

Something of that particularism will no doubt continue into the 21st century. Fortunately, there are no signs that mass culture can exclude from the spiritual field a vital minority—writer/philosophers like Peter Høeg. They carry on the spirit of search, they seek to embrace the whole, whatever the trends in the fashionable mainstream. They try to awaken the world to sensibility. In other words, they dare to oppose evil.

The novelty in *Smilla's Sense of Snow* means that a lot has been borrowed from modernism between two World Wars. Høeg avoids a linear, logically developing story, and avoids clearly defining his characters. Consciousness has been fragmented, but from fragments a new whole is built. One discovers in Høeg's novel feminist features, as the narrating main character is Smilla Qaavigaaq Jaspersen, a young woman born from the union of a Greenlandic native woman hunter and Danish university professor, well educated in natural sciences and determined to oppose male tyranny and fraud. In the final ship adventure, fighting alone against a gang of smugglers she manages to survive.

The mysterious island called Gela Alta alludes to science fiction, for instance, with the motifs of Jules Verne's 19th-century novel *The Mysterious Island* (1870). In fact, in Høeg's novel there is some talk about Verne and other science fiction authors.

Yet a realistic dimension prevails in the novel. Høeg depicts a world that is fully known to us, without trying to flee from its faultiness to the past or to future illusions. In the history of literature, realism has always been closely bound to criticism. In the case of Høeg, this aspect is first of all revealed in a nation's self-criticism, relying on a concrete analysis of Danishness. In Estonian literature of my days, only a few exceptional writers have dared to make attempts in this direction.

Naturally, in our case it would be much more difficult to write such novels. Our history has hardly varied from having been trodden under the feet of bigger nations (by the way, the Danes included). Therefore, our novels have been directed against those invaders-foreigners, without asking about our own faults. Instead, we have been inclined and accustomed to idealize our own nation. The work of A.H. Tammsaare and Jaan Kross has been nation-building literature. Its philosophy, whose background is an Enlightenment utopia of reason, has been by now exhausted. It is clearly insufficient for explaining the world at the start of the 21st century.

Høeg, a new Danish Hamlet, however, presses his finger exactly on a Danish abscess, but one with a universality. The epoch of idealizing science has irreversibly come to its end. Science is religion—but without the sacred germ that still vegetated in the earlier religious conscience. On the contrary, modern science participates most directly in the dirty business of power and in spreading evil on the earth. Høeg is bold enough to express the fact by means of the images of his novel.

Yet mere criticism from outside would not weigh much. Yuri Lotman once mentioned that "a novel needs idle talk." Indeed, it needs idle talk, lighter speech, and it also needs poetry. Høeg is not deprived of these talents. Nonetheless, when one is set to write a *sur*-technical novel, then an inevitable requirement is to know the cardinal operations of technique, to understand science as one of the *ur*-instincts of Western male. Only then is one prepared to reach philosophic conclusions. Høeg has perfectly managed it.

LETTER 8

THERE ARE NUMEROUS EXAMPLES OF noble-hearted men, sensible to the historical injustice caused by their own gender to women, trying to voice in their works if not a direct protest, at least compassion. Calderón went further than Lope de Vega or Shakespeare in this respect. He not only showed in his plays women as victims of physical violation on part of males. He almost grotesquely exaggerated in his dramas (like *El médico de su honra, A secreto agravio, secreta venganza, El pintor de su honra*, and others) the code of honour established by men. Even the slightest attempt to offend a woman's "honour" (in reality a family's appearance or prestige) incited bloody vengeance from the "offended" males. Calderón thus showed women as daily harassed by the cruellest psychological oppression, which was even worse than sexual offense. It deprived women of any freedom as individuals. Women were manipulated by males and made perfect prisoners, both at home and in society.

By means of an intensive exaggeration, Tirso de Molina in his *El burlador de Sevilla y convidado de piedra* denounced the same kind of injustice done to woman: Marriages were contracted at the court; if some obstacles (like offending somebody's "honour") emerged, immediately other combinations of marriages were settled. The principle of "compensation" was made to work with such efficiency that in Tirso de Molina's play those ridiculed are above all males plotting in the court marriages of their daughters, with the consent of the king. In the final episode, when all Don Juan's sins are revealed, the king, a good-natured and generous man, appears as a perfect simpleton: He does not know anything that really happens in his country. In a number of comedies (such as *La dama duende*, perhaps his best-known farcical comedy), Calderón makes women stand forth as main characters: Their initiatives in the plots reveal them as witty-spirited, intellectually more alert than men who are ridiculed, incapable of finding out truth amid a mess of "appearances" and "essences."

In *Life Is a Dream*, one of his greatest European philosophical dramas, Calderón showed by the example of one of the main characters, Rosaura, that woman can intellectually equal man: Her arguing in defense of her honour, justifying revenge, is the same conceptually elaborated language of males who keep society under rational control, depriving individuals, above all women, of their freedom. However, Calderón hardly approved equalizing woman with man and thus intensifying male tyranny in society. In *No hay burlas con el amor*, a light comedy, quite serious issues in gender relationships, not at all "overcome" by the start of the 21st century, are involved. A learned young lady demonstrates there her intellectual superiority, as regards men. Both she and her solicitor try to take love as something inferior, from the point of view of intellect and science. However, when she really falls in love, intellect must give up its mind-games. It does not provide a remedy when one comes to genuinely existential choices, determining one's fate in the limited time lapse of an individual life.

In literature created by persons younger than myself, the vision of Peter Høeg in his novel *Smilla's Sense of Snow* transcends a narrowly intimate inter-gender perspective (much exploited in the novels by women authors of our time), to expose, even though in part in the framework of a semi-fantastic adventure narrative, universal processes that may easily lead, with the consent of most of us, to life's disappearance from the earth. Høeg shows how science, the reign of the male, has come to form a vast anonymous structure which, in consequence of men's greed for material welfare and their thirst for power, hides the most atrocious crimes against humanity.

Smilla is a brave woman shown in her individual fight against a male-dominated world of corruption and crime, in the name of preserving nature.

The novel has an happy end, its outcome could be proper to a utopia. Smilla becomes a superwoman, defeating in the final battle supermen embodying alienated and corrupt power. Or who knows, maybe also Høeg, like Thomas More long before him, hints at some solutions that at present may seem to us utopian, but in the longer run of history come true?

* * *

But I now leave aside the noble-spirited male writers, defending women, to reflect in the remaining part of this letter on women who have not conformed to the role of being defended and treated with compassion, but have become themselves active creators of a different philosophy, to bring more balance to the mind-world unilaterally dominated in history by male ratiocinations.

Women's interior world began to be revealed from their own point of view in the work of some noblewomen of France, your country, in the 17th century. One of the most admirable prose novels, *Princess de la Clèves*, still enjoying success among the readers of my day, was published by Madame de La Fayette in 1678. It is possible that she might have read a short narrative by Cervantes, *El celoso extremeño*, which has a similar plot, with a parallel unexpected final turn. After a long series of love torments to which the main characters are submitted, La Fayette makes her protagonist, a young married woman called Princess de la Clèves, when she at last is virtually free to marry to her lover, take a different path: She decides to spend the rest of her days in a cloister, thus escaping the earthy world with its passions.

Something similar occurred to Sor Juana Inés de la Cruz (2nd half of the 17th century), a young talented Mexican woman in the vast European dominion and periphery, the continent of America. Very early she revealed her many-sided talents, being equally capable in the field of literature and sciences. She was bored by the hypocrisy and corruption reigning in the world governed by men and decided to become a nun. There, too, she had troubles and conflicts with her male superiors. However, she managed to write some plays and poems, in which she voiced her strong protest against men's falsity, vanity and corruption. Thus the first and last stanzas of one of her best-known poems read as follows:

> Hombres necios que acusáis
> a la mujer sin razón,
> sin ver que sois la occasion
> de lo mismo que culpáis;
>
> _ _ _ _ _ _ _ _ _ _ _ _ _ _
>
> Bien con muchas armas fundo
> que lidia vuestra arrogancia;
> pues en promesa e instancia,
> juntáis diablo, carne y mundo.

> Vain males who accuse
> woman without reason,
> without seeing that you yourselves are the cause
> of what you blame them for
>
> _ _ _ _ _ _ _ _ _ _ _ _ _ _ _ _ _ _
>
> I know well those many arms
> by which your arrogance fights;
> because in promise and instance
> you unite the devil, the flesh and the world.

The poem, at least for me, is the first feminist manifesto written in the West by a woman herself.

* * *

The 18th century, known to the West as the Enlightenment, witnessed the rise of knowledge and sciences in Western centres. As sciences were in ascent, the symbol of traditional and conservative knowledge, the Church, came under attack. Thus in an unprecedented move, the most combative unit of Catholicism, the Jesuits, were banished in France, Spain and Portugal, so that they had to flee Europe. They were repelled also from South America, where they had become quite influential as defenders of the rights of the indigenous population in the Spanish and Portuguese colonies.

European males were in the vanguard of the rise of sciences. First encyclopaedic dictionaries, attempting to gather all the existing knowledge about the world, were prepared in France, followed later by similar efforts in other countries. The Enlightenment pretended to envisage man's liberation by means of science and knowledge from a blind and dogmatic past, dominated by hereditary nobility and the church. At this point, culture and civilization seemed to be identical in their aspiration to enlighten humanity's path to a more just and freer future. Women had little part if any in this process, though the keywords of the French revolution at the end of the 18th century (liberty, equality, fraternity) seemed to promise a future world in which all citizens could live according to these noble principles.

However, I think one of the keywords, "fraternity," betrays the real essence of the historical turn. It was not "sorority," but just "fraternity": The new freedoms and equality were meant first and foremost for men, not for women. Even one of the most radical among the Enlightenment thinkers, Jean-Jacques Rousseau, who became famous for his passionate call for a return to nature, allotted woman merely a secondary role in the new imagined world of free citizens. It is quite an eloquent fact that in the very heart of Western Europe, Switzerland, a country famous for its banks and monetary operations, following democratic principles, neutral in both 20th-century world wars, women obtained for the first time partial suffrage only in 1971.

Whatever its contradictions and deficiencies, the revolution led in your country by such men as Robespierre, Saint-Just, and Danton, shook like an earthquake the whole Western world. North America contributed to the turn toward new liberties when, after battles with England, the United States was born, with a manifesto of human rights accompanying its birth. It claimed faithfulness to the principles of democracy from the very beginning of its existence. Naturally, to put these principles into practice, hard battles were still to follow (above all the U.S. civil war, in the latter half of the 19th century).

* * *

The Enlightenment ideology, with its strongly idealized and exaggerated principles of human rationality and materialistic goals, had inevitably to feed a conflict within itself. It contradicted culture and creativity, allies of nature and beauty. The conflict culminated with unprecedented power at the end of the 18th century, in parallel with revolutionary developments. A new type of culture, known as Romanticism, emerged in Europe. Enlightenment had fed it, but Romanticism was not its natural child but a bastard. It did not look for its sources in the classical age—though it did not ignore them either—but turned to the obscure and anonymous popular and traditional poetry of the Middle Ages, to some extent despised already in the Renaissance, but completely neglected, as inferior and "low," during the Neoclassical era.

In the Western "centre," the boldest voice of dissidence diverging from Enlightenment rationalism belonged to Rousseau, philosopher and writer. His call for a return to nature and natural simplicity, along with his grudge against the fruits of civilization, was heard all over Europe. He became the main ideologist of the French revolution, revered by its leaders like Robespierre. Rousseau's message reached the widest European public, precisely because he was not a professional philosopher, but first and foremost a talented writer who could present his ideas through sensual images. He praised human feelings and religion inspired by nature. The main audience of his bulky sentimental novel in letters, *Julie, ou la Nouvelle Héloïse* was women. His Émile was not a philosophical treatise, but a discourse in the vein of your *Essays*.

In Émile, Rousseau created a character, an ideally educated young man named Émile, but he did not develop the work into a novel either. By the example of Émile's moral formation, presented in a language easily accessible to any reader, Rousseau demonstrated eloquently and convincingly that civilization and culture based on knowledge and science would lead humankind ever farther from nature, naturalness, and all moral good, of which the basis, he claimed, could only be nature. According to Rousseau, growing amid nature and in a natural environment, away from the vices procreated and fed by civilization, humans can only be morally good, virtuous. Rousseau also envisaged nature as the noblest source of religion.

Obviously, in developing such ideas Rousseau was indebted to your *Essays*. Especially in those essays where you speak of the South American indigenous communities. You claim that illiterate indigenous people, without reading books, without philosophical speculations, and apart from any other sources of Western civilization, were morally superior to Westerners, deeply corrupted in all spheres of activity.

Almost simultaneously with Rousseau—a dissident acting in the "centre," a strong voice of dissidence came from Germany, a big fragmented nation that had been a Renaissance "periphery," but as the 18th century progressed, had increased spectacularly its philosophical contribution to the Enlightenment. The main German ideologist of Romanticism was Johann Gottfried Herder who in his younger days worked as a pastor, belonging at the same time to the mason's movement in Riga, the capital of Estonia's neighbouring country, Latvia, in Europe's deep "periphery." There Herder wrote his first influential philosophical essays, under the title of *Kritische Wälder*, published in 1769.

Herder claimed that the sources of Europe's greatest poetry had to be found in oral creation of its peoples, the works of those closest to nature, and, more concretely, in the traditional poetry created anonymously by bards like the medieval Celtic poet Ossian, whose songs, evoked and reproduced by the Scotsman James Macpherson, he considered equal in their cultural value to the greatest epics produced by antiquity. Herder called Spanish late medieval romances the "Spanish *Iliad*." He highly appreciated medieval anonymous epics, under whose influence, in his older days, he himself wrote a longer poem, *Cid*.

Thus Herder destroyed at the root the idea of progress, of gradually achieved higher perfection in culture, in unison with the development of civilization. On the contrary, he showed that no culture can claim superiority to other types of culture. The idea of modernity's superiority over tradition, strongly advocated since the Neo-classical era in France, was turned upside down.

In full accord with your intuition in *Essays*, Herder claimed that the closer cultural creation is to nature and the senses, the sources of human feelings and the *ur-Sparche*, to be found in ancient oral tradition above all, the more completely it can reflect human consciousness in its integrity and totality.

He was fully aware of the inevitable course of the *ur-Sprache*'s disintegration, as the result of Western civilizing process. Yet he was convinced that parts of human culture, especially poetry, can carry on the original integral sensibility of the *ur*-language. Thus in *Stimmen der Völker in Liedern* (1778–1779), his anthology of traditional poetry of different European peoples, representing bigger and smaller nations alike (Spaniards, Portuguese, German, but also Estonians, Latvians and Lithuanians), he included also some poems by Johann Wolfgang von Goethe, a versatile genius, who created lyrical poems imitating traditional medieval poetry.

Later, when Herder had passed away, Goethe who excelled also in his philosophically-inclined essays and letters, coined the term *Weltliteratur*. He was influenced by Herder's idea of a new universality, in which the "other," defined from the point of view of the rationally most developed "first," virtually became inexistent, unnecessary. All cultures and their carriers, big and small nations likewise, can contribute by their literary creation to world literature. Every literature can be a subject, "self." Through the outstanding part of national literatures, which ideally would become the heritage of the entire world, different nations establish a spiritual-mental dialogue. As Goethe said, even if nations cannot love each other, world literature can at least contribute to an increased mutual understanding and tolerance.

* * *

Thus in Romantic culture a great effort was made to merge the sentimental and the mental. A huge "leap" was made toward abolishing the mental tyranny established in cultural creation by men. All nations and peoples, males and females, civilized as well as "under-civilized" peoples came to be considered equal in their creative potentiality. In the radically renewed atmosphere women started to reveal their many talents ever more courageously, especially in literary creation. To avoid scandals, some of the first eminent woman writers published their work under male names (thus George Sand became the literary pseudonym of Lucile Aurore Dupin, while also the English pioneering trio, the Brontë sisters, published their first novels under male names; later, George Eliot was the pseudonym of Mary Ann Evans, and Fernán Caballero of Cecilia Böhl de Faber, in Spain). However, once the pioneering books had been published and met favourably by readers, women became increasingly visible in Europe's literary scene.

Annex 7

Harriet Beecher Stowe: *Uncle Tom's Cabin* (1852)

CONTEMPORARY LITERARY THEORETICIANS WHO WASTE a lot of energy on analyzing narrative technique and mind games of novels often forget that writers seldom create their works merely to display their technique. Literature is sociology, philosophy, and psychology of its own kind—in the best case all three together. But literature's unique contribution is that writers, sensible minds, capable of feeling the depths of life and spirit, can transmit the conclusions of a sociologist, a philosopher, and a psychologist in such a way that they do not remain in the narrow circle of science but can awaken to consciousness a broad human audience.

Among the various causes of social turns and changes, literature has never been of secondary importance. Some historians of our day believe that the novel *Uncle Tom's Cabin* by Harriet Beecher Stowe might have incited the start of American Civil War (1861–1865), which dealt a most serious blow to slavery and trafficking in human beings, which until then had been considered in the West as a matter of course. It is also supposed that, after a public address by Stowe, Great Britain abstained from intervening on the side of the Southern states.

Naturally, behind these developments were the great French Revolution and Romanticism. It was at the same time the most decisive breakthrough in the direction of liberating woman as a spiritual being. Along with Byron, Shelley, Victor Hugo, Dickens, Heine, and many men seeking social justice, women appeared on the literary scene. With Nordic women in their vanguard, by the end of the 19th century they formed an entire constellation which has left its indelible footprint in world literature.

It is not mere chance that among the first to raise their voice of protest against the racism that sanctioned slavery of Africans were women—who themselves for centuries had suffered from tyranny and misogyny. Although Beecher Stowe's *Uncle Tom's Cabin* was to become the first world-famous novel to pillory the slavery of black people, ten years earlier a similar protest was voiced in a novel written in Spanish. The author was a young Cuban-Spanish woman, Gertrudis Gómez de Avellaneda. In her short novel *Sab* (1841), she depicted black, brown, and white women equally as victims of the historical violence of Western white men.

In Cuba where in those times traffic in slaves was still legal, Gómez de Avellaneda's book was banned. The fate of Stowe's *Uncle Tom's Cabin* in the Southern U.S. states was similar: People reading or spreading the work were severely punished.

Condemning traffic in human beings and slavery is not the only value of *Uncle Tom's Cabin*. The action of the novel is closely bound with a religious background. Stowe grew up in the earnest spirit of Protestantism. In her novel she shows in a positive light the religious sect of the Quakers. At the same time it was impossible to attribute slavery in the Southern states to Catholicism. As a result, Stowe allusively sets the Christianity condemning slavery against Protestant opportunism, without whose tacit approval southern violence against black people could never have taken root.

The novel emphasizes motherly love and the historical opposition of women to the world of violence created by men. It is the message of Eliza who flees with her little son, but most female characters of the work refer to the same, though in different shades. The martyr Tom is loved from her whole heart by Eva, the little daughter of a slaveholder. Letting Eva die of an illness, Stowe generates her message of nature's purity and sacredness, of love—both in natural or Christian mean-ing—as the main need and truth of existence.

One should not underestimate literature's impact. If Finnish schoolchildren had discussed in their lessons of literature the rel-evance of *Uncle Tom's Cabin* to our time, could the high-school bloodshed of Jokela, in 2007, have been averted?

LETTER 9

INDEED, WOMEN SEEM LESS INCLINED than men to apply in literature elaborate artifice and technique. Thus extensive end-rhymed genres, like epics, probably have not been the exclusive domain of male creators only because of social conditions—beyond doubt, historically favouring men, but also because of women's natural distrust of the artificially technical. In Estonia, women have been among the most versatile translators of extensive prose novels. They have also translated poetry, but overwhelmingly have avoided translating poetry employing strict end-rhymes. When rhyme patterns are loose, as for instance in Estonian traditional folk-poetry, women have wonderfully revealed their poetic talent. Relying on other, more natural elements of artistic creation, like alliteration, assonances, parallelisms, and repetitions, they created in the past a vast treasury of our folk-poetry, incredibly rich in psychological understanding.

Roughly, the middle of the 19th century meant in Western literature a definite turn to prose forms. Especially in the European "centre," long verse narrative was gradually abandoned, replaced by the novel. Also drama, a literary genre presupposing particular technical skills, came increasingly to be written in prose. Thus Henrik Ibsen, the great Norwegian playwright, whose work reflected a substantially new attitude towards women, and was pioneering in its psychological scrutiny of modern society, wrote his first plays (including one of his most famous, *Peer Gynt*), still under the spell of romantic tradition, in verse, but nearly all of his later work was in prose.

When the first outstandingly talented women writers emerged in 19th-century European literature, strict end-rhymes were still widely cultivated in poetry, which was the domain of males. However, from the 1810s and 1820s, when Walter Scott employed prose for extensive historical narratives, written earlier almost exclusively in verse forms, often with end-rhymes, a change started. (Madame La Fayette was among the remote predecessors of the historical novel in prose, but the genre as such emerged no earlier than the 19th century.) In the early 1830s, George Sand published her first novel, *Indiana*. It was a great success, encouraging its author to follow her literary career. Subsequently, she became an extremely productive novelist and prose writer, rivalling in the volume of her work if not Balzac, at least other giant writers of her lifetime such as Hugo, Mérimée, or Stendhal.

Indiana's tremendous success no doubt was due to a radically new point of view. The main character, Indiana, largely coinciding with the author herself, told about her yearning for an ideal love and her anguish in the materialistic, vulgar city, subject to the scheming of vicious males. The novel was written from the perspective of the humiliated "other." The role of the narrator changed at the root. What had been "other" suddenly became "self," with its strong individual features, and with a sensibility for intimate details that often had been hidden from the eyes of males. In comparison with *Indiana*, female characters in the novels of Walter Scott and the pioneering American novelist James Fenimore Cooper started to look utterly pale. The greatest of French male novelists (Balzac, Stendhal, Zola, Flaubert), relying both on personal experience with women and on the long French cultural and literary tradition of psychological investigation, could brilliantly evoke aspects of women in their work, but they too admired George Sand.

The same was the source of main novelty in the work of the Brontë sisters, Charlotte and Emily. Love was presented from a woman's point of view, comprising a "self" not at all inferior or less individualized than the "self" in the similar narratives of males. In parallel with Sand's *Indiana*, Charlotte Brontë's *Jane Eyre* not only looked for happiness in her intimate life, but also aspired to manifest her individuality as a person, in the complicated set of social relations. Sand wrote much more than Charlotte or Emily Brontë, and lost in her later novels something of *Indiana*'s intimate spontaneity. She became perhaps too obsessed by the idealistic projects launched by the noble male spirits of her time. Therefore, the plots and the final solutions of her novels tended to be artificially conceived, submitted to rational scheming. However, some of these works, like *Consuelo*, can be read as an energetic manifesto of the ideal of women's emancipation and liberation as creative personalities.

Passion combined with sensibility for intimate details became from the very beginning of women's major debut their main asset in literary expression. However, the women writers of those times, all keen readers of novels from their early girlhood, had learned from the art and technique employed by men in their narratives. Thus Emily Brontë's *Wuthering Heights* is an outstanding work not only because it transmits love passion as a mythically fatal *ur*-call penetrating humans along with the rest of living nature. The story became magically shaped because like Cervantes in his *Don Quixote* and also Walter Scott in some of his novels (e.g. *Rob Roy*), Emily Brontë skilfully introduced an intermediating narrator, thus providing the narrated world more autonomy and freedom than in stories narrated directly by the authors of the work.

Women novelists were among the pioneers in introducing the point of view of the social, racial, and cultural "other."

La Gaviota (1849), the debut novel written initially in French by Fernán Caballero (in fact, a young German woman Cecilia Böhl de Faber, born of a German father and a Spanish mother) introduced a double point of view, both from "inside" (Spanish popular culture, folksongs, bull-fighting) and "outside" (of a foreign visitor, cultural "other"). It was a pioneering work, overcoming the overwhelmingly exclusive perspective from "inside" Spanish society, which had dominated in Spanish literature in the 18th century and still prevailed for the greater part of the 19th century. It revealed an early philosophical approach to reality in Spanish literature.

"Own" and "alien" established an incipient dialogue. Half a century later, a similar openness to the "outside" was among the main factors of the emergence of philosophically minded literary work by the so-called *Generación del '98* (Unamuno, Ortega y Gasset, Baroja, Azorín, Antonio Machado, J.R. Jiménez and others). It brought about a major renovation and rise in Spanish culture. That generation, like the following one, the poetic group calling itself *Generación del '27* (including among its most famous members Federico García Lorca and Vicente Aleixandre) comprised the work of men, first and foremost. Yet without their openness to women and their acceptance of an emancipating gendered "other," these generations would hardly have obtained their glories in Spanish culture.

* * *

Also in Europe's northern "periphery" women writers, as if by a sudden "explosion," became spectacularly active and visible. In Estonia, Lydia Koidula (born as Lydia Jannsen, daughter of an Estonian father and a German mother) won a permanent place in the memory of her nation by her patriotic poems, which, far more than similar poems written by males, have been absorbed into the inner self of the Estonians, not left only on its surface, dominated by the political scheming of males.

Here lies the difference. Koidula's work was a brilliant proof that nations were not merely the result of the intellectual scheming of a minority of its educated people. Nations breathe by their natural language. Poetry that concentrates in its images that breathing, drawing on the past and seeking at the same time to envisage for a nation a freer future, does not exercise its influence merely on people's brains. First and foremost, it addresses people's feelings. Some of Koidula's poems, turned into songs by talented composers, especially "My Fatherland Is My Love" (*Mu isamaa on minu arm*), are known by every Estonian, because they have been presented at the traditional all-nation song-festivals and echoed all over the country since the 1860s.

If Estonians by their nature tend to be rationally-minded individualists, at least once every year, when choirs from all corners of the country come together to sing such songs as Koidula's, they become united by feeling. Or, as the great poet Juhan Liiv has said in one of his early "thought-poems": "Aspiration separates the world. / Feeling unites it."

The pathos of Koidula's poems was directed against foreign domination in Estonia, especially that of the Baltic German rulers who had exploited and humiliated her nation for long centuries, keeping Estonian peasants in anonymous obscurity as serfs, depriving them of their most elementary rights as individuals. At the same time Koidula, like other Estonian intellectuals of the "national awakening" (who in those times all knew German almost as well as their native Estonian), was inspired by some of the most passionate calls for freedom reaching the European periphery from Germany itself. Thus Koidula was among the early Estonian translators of Heinrich Heine's poetry. She modelled a number of her poems on forms from German poetry, but leant them by means of her feminine consciousness and a skilful use of her Estonian language an emotional gravity that they seldom had in the original performance by German authors.

Besides her poetic work, she also wrote some prose plays, and was among the initiators of the Estonian national theatre. In a story, "The Last Inca of Peru," adapted from a German work, "Huaskar," by W.O. von Horn, Koidula evoked the personality of the Spanish dissenting priest Bartolomé de las Casas, the boldest defender of the human rights of the American indigenous population, in the days of the Spanish conquest of the New World. She thus created an emotional bridge from the huge American periphery of the West to its European obscure periphery, generating a cry for the freedom of the racial and social "other."

In a milder way, a woman's lyrical voice emerged at the same time from the other edge of Europe's periphery, Galicia. Amid the overwhelming majority of male creators, the Galician Rosalía de Castro restored to Iberian literature of the times a late Romantic lyric sensibility. She was not as directly outspoken as Koidula on the patriotic issues: The historical backgrounds of Estonians and Galicians have been notably different. However, just like Lydia Koidula in Estonia, Rosalía de Castro provided some part of her poems with a special intimate sensibility for the beauty of her homeland and its nature, not frequent at all in the work of male poets.

In the Latin American periphery, following the Mexican Sor Juana Inés de la Cruz and the Cuban Gertrudis Gómez de Avellaneda, the pioneering women's voices of the colonial period, the early independence of Latin American countries brought to the literary scene women such as the Peruvian Clorinda Matto de Turner. She was among the first authors on the continent to protest in her novels—of which the best known is *Aves sin nido* (1889)—against social and racial exploitation of the indigenous population, as well as against priests' immorality. In a time when business, industry, and the church all were managed by males, Matto de Turner's literary work delivered a courageous outcry of justice against the tyranny of the traditional "first gender," white males.

* * *

North America followed a different type of literary tradition, one predominantly proceeding from English literature. The ever more powerfully emerging "periphery," after breaking away from Great Britain and establishing its independence, was by the start of the 20th century to become itself one of the main Western "centres". From that intense intersection or border zone between a potentially huge "periphery" and the European-British "centre," the first deeply original voice in literature belonged to Walt Whitman. His pioneering role in world poetry is not only manifest in his vigorous call for democracy, the equality of all peoples, races, and genders, but also in his strong will to write in free verse without end-rhymes.

He surely had influential predecessors in early English Romanticism, including the artist-poet, the prophet of humanity's total emancipation, William Blake. In Germany, too, early in the 19th century, Heinrich Heine wrote some cycles of his poetry either in loosely end-rhymed patterns of traditional folk-poetry or in unrhymed free verse. Then, though, it was a rare exception. In the European "centre," the French symbolists, contemporaries of Whitman, soon imposed their taste for the delicate end-rhymed patterns overwhelmingly applied by Western poets until WWI. Also, the first major talent in American poetry, E.A. Poe, himself under the influence of the mystical current of English romantic poetry (especially Coleridge), wrote all his work in regular end-rhymed stanzas. Whitman's stubborn decision to write exclusively in free unrhymed verse laid the main basis in world poetry for a radical break with end-rhyme and a crucial turn towards free rhythms and verses.

The first gifted North American woman poet, Emily Dickinson, was not at all known in her lifetime. Her fame was established posthumously. She was a contemporary of Whitman, but in her very short and concise poems she relied on loose rhymes, as was the case with Heine in Germany and Liiv in Estonia. In contrast with Whitman's energetic masculinity and unreserved openness to the whole world, Dickinson achieved in her poems astonishing intimacy and delicacy of feeling and thought, something that was almost unknown in the Western "centre." She too advocated freedom and turning to nature, but she appeared philosophically more mature than most male poets, who often have had a tendency either to naive idealism or to grim pessimism.

While Whitman only in the latter part of his work began to realize that the bodily "greatness" of his country, the U.S., could also bear in itself seeds of a deep moral fall, Dickinson from the very start of her work knew too well that in the end what matters is one's life as an individual, conditioned by the limits of life, as well as by love, not given to everyone in equal doses. In the maturity of her thought she closely resembled our Estonian Juhan Liiv. The extraordinary delicacy of the poetic expression of both has closer parallels in Eastern poetry than in the mainstream of Western poetic tradition.

* * *

In the great political-ideological and social turmoil of the fin de siècle, women writers came to manifest their vigorous presence in Europe's Northern "periphery," Scandinavia. Perhaps the brightest talents among them were the Swedish Selma Lagerlöf, the Norwegian Sigrid Undset, and the Swedish-Finnish Edith Södergran. All three voiced protest against social norms and prohibitions based on male rationality. They sought more freedom for women, as well as more social justice. Södergran, working under the influence of Friedrich Nietzsche, wrote in her poems about universal love that would emancipate the whole world, freeing humankind, body and soul.

Erotic and passionate love, free from moral chains, was also sung by other "peripheral" woman poets, such as the Uruguayan Juana de Ibarbourou or the Estonian Marie Under. Among winners of the Nobel Prize for literature, awarded to 108 writers since the start of the 20th century, women writers still are in a clear minority, only 12, against 96 men. The first woman to receive it was Selma Lagerlöf, who by 1909 had become widely known especially as a writer for children and youth. Among five women winners of Nobel Prize for literature by the middle of the 20th century, the only poet was the Chilean Gabriela Mistral (Nobel Prize in 1945, the year marking the end of WWII). Indeed, women have been largely neglected by the award-giving Swedish Academy.

* * *

However, there are sure signs of change since the start of the 1990s, coinciding not only with the collapse of the world's greatest communist empire, the USSR (which at least in its official propaganda advocated social justice in the world), but also with a powerful rise of feminism, not at all limited to the West. Feminism is rapidly extending to other parts of the world, even in Moslem countries where traditionally women have been humiliated and kept in darkness by men.

Maybe the world operates by a mechanism of interior compensation? The communist empire of the 20th century was a dictatorship, an autocracy, beyond any doubt. It deprived its population of individual liberties, choices, and initiatives, an essential need of any adult person. Yet the officially proclaimed moral goals of socialism and communism were noble. They hardly differed from Christian philosophy, paradoxically denied and rejected by communist ideologists. People's friendship, equality of man and woman, possibilities for education and culture for all members of a society, mutual cooperation and aid, caring for the "other," not letting anyone suffer from hunger, etc.—what was wrong in these official slogans of socialism?

For a wide sector of people in the West and in societies based on capitalism, the "second world" embodied by the USSR and its satellite socialist countries meant an alternative, something different from the capitalist market-economy with its crudely materialistic goals. Naturally, often these people let themselves be duped by the highly astute official propaganda-machine of the USSR. In reality, the "noble" empire was full of moral defects and corruption. After the collapse of the communist empire many people in the West, not only those who idealized the USSR, started to feel a kind of a moral-ideological void, as the possible imaginary alternative was destroyed.

Feminism transcends political-ideological barriers of both antagonistic systems, capitalism and socialism. In fact these systems were built by males and relied basically on their power strategies. Once in power, there was little difference between "capitalist" and "socialist" males: They became corrupt and vicious, not caring at all for the "other," or caring for it only in their hypocritical oratory. Thus feminism, whatever its extremes since the end part of the 20th century, has become a substantial moral movement towards nobler goals than those which have traditionally dominated in societies built by males.

Women are slower in their action, not inclined to scheme violent revolutions. However, by advancing steadily and firmly, they may reach objectives that in the long run can cause important shifts in the quality of life on the earth.

In the context of 20th-century modernist literature, it is a significant fact that, although women definitely shared some of the basic philosophy of male modernists, such as liberation from the dictatorship of reason, introduction of freer forms of expression, they seldom became so fond of formal experiments as men or indulged in intellectual or verbal games. Although Virginia Woolf, a lonely woman in the company of Western modernist writers, did introduce some of the most important novelties in her art of narration, she did not approve James Joyce's sexual dreams or his attempts to make language itself the main subject and character of his novels. Even liberation from the dictatorship of reason tends to be governed in male creators by strong intellectual commandments. They were the main schemers of surrealist manifestos. The greatest among the poets between two world wars, such as the Spaniard Federico García Lorca, never approved of the principle of "psychical automatism," establish by French surrealists in their manifesto.

Automatism, as such, contradicts any great poetic creation. No principles or rules, invented by intellect, can be applied to poetry. When preparing a major anthology of American poetry in Estonian translation, I came across the work of Amy Lowell. Critics have defined her as one of the American modernist poets. However, I found in Lowell's poems a deep distrust as regards the stormy and violent social revolution in which strong males were engaged in her time. Women somehow intuitively understand that any too-violent imposition of ideas on nature, however noble the goals expressed in manifestos, leads to the destruction of some of the essential facets of beauty and sensibility in our selves, in our basic individual existence.

In any case it is a highly eloquent fact that, from 1991 to 2011, that means during a lapse of scarce 20 years, no fewer than six women writers have been awarded the Nobel Prize for literature. Thus merely in two recent decades women writers have been honoured as much as during the preceding nine decades. Indeed, it is a most obvious sign of change in gender relations in the spiritual-mental field, reflecting broader shifts in the entire spectrum of human activities in the world.

Annex 8

J.M.G. Le Clézio: *Desert* (1980)2[*]
To Feel the Sea, the Desert, the "Other"

THREE STORIES IN THE BOOK bearing in Estonian translation the title *The Boy Who Had Never Seen the Sea*, by the Nobel Prize winner Jean Marie Gustave Le Clézio, clearly belong to children's literature. In the first story, "Lullaby," the main character, a teenage girl, decides that she will no longer go to school. Instead she goes to the sea, to seaside cliffs, to a mountain where she finds an abandoned house called Charisma. In the second story, "The Boy Who Had Never Seen the Sea," the main character Daniel leaves his school and home, without any wish to return. In the third story, "The Mountain of the Living God," the author describes the experiences of a boy named Jon on a volcanic mountain.

All three stories belong to Le Clézió's collection *Mondo and Other Stories* (1978). On the back cover of the translated Estonian book one reads that the stories are often included in French school readers. They could be taken also to our Estonian school reading books, without any fear that the reluctance of Lullaby and Daniel, as regards going to school, would spread a negative example. All three stories end peacefully, in a reconciliatory mood. It appears that Lullaby's strict teacher of mathematics, Filippi, whose formulas made the girl

---

[*] The present essay was first published in Estonian in the cultural weekly *Sirp*, 8.V 2009.

defiant, secretly loves the sea. Lullaby returns to school and home. Similarly, after wandering on the mountain, Jon returns to his home farm. The reader and his schoolmates never know about the fate of Daniel, but at the end of the story it appears that Daniel, a lonely boy, has still left an impression on his companions. Even more: As accomplices, in their interior they share Daniel's dream about liberation. They try to imagine in what distant seas Daniel could be sailing.

The author explains about Daniel: "The earthly things like shops, cars, music, films, and naturally, also school and studying, did not interest him." It is fairly difficult to imagine how at our Estonian pragmatically-inclined schools, where as it seems to be, pupils as well as teachers are excited by "earthly things"—on which, as it is generally believed, depends everyone's success and future—would receive Le Clézio's stories. I guess that for a small minority of our schoolchildren they would certainly have a purifying effect. But would there be enough teachers ready to invite the budding souls to catharsis? Would there be enough will and determination to resist the contemporary mainstream, unambiguously based on the formula of earthly success?

Quite surely cathartic qualities are not absent from our own Estonian literature, whether written for children or adults. For instance, in Ain Kaalep's book *Jumalatosin* ('God's Dozen'), there is a story titled "Niobe and the Ladybird." Our humanist writer of the older generation shows by a beautiful image what catharsis means. Pain that had infiltrated into the heart of a little girl by the story about Niobe, told by the girl's father, is carried away by a lady bird. Kaalep explains: "What was left in the heart of the girl, after the ladybird had carried away pain, was called 'catharsis' by Aristotle, in ancient Athens."

Nature took away pain and purified the soul. The same is the main idea of Le Clézio's stories. Or rather, it is the main feeling, because manifesting explicitly ideas would contradict Le Clézio's philosophy. Let senses talk with senses. They, whose senses are open, will also understand the idea. An idea in a symbiosis with senses is always richer and deeper than ideas which have been torn apart from life's totality and have been presented in their nakedness.

In my recent writing I have been suspicious of centric discourses, either in theory or in literature and, especially, of the imitation of mainstreams at "edges" (like today's Eastern Europe, Estonia included). Yet one should not interpret it as a kind of underestimation, on my part, of centres' potentiality. On the contrary, it also remains a fact that explosively powerful defiance against the mainstream and the defense of "edges" have often departed from strong and ample spirituality at the very centres. As self-defence of the "edges," similar defiance tends to die down, stumbling against simple language barriers.

I have in mind Le Clézio's fellow-countrymen from the times of the Renaissance, François Rabelais and Michel de Montaigne. The former in his book *Gargantua and Pantagruel* let sexual-primitive nature turn upside down scholasticism and dogmatism based on officially consecrated writing. The features of scholastic thinking have, in France, especially, taken deep roots. Even French postmodern theories have not been redeemed from its impact. More thoroughly than any European thinker before him, Montaigne validated the cultural and natural "other," as equal to "first" and "self," and even superior to them, as regards virtue. He shook occidental anthropocentrism and logo-centrism much more powerfully than Jacques Derrida, the "father" of postmodernism, in our near past, ever managed.

For that reason I was pleased to learn that Le Clézio was awarded the Nobel. He is a spiritual heir of Rabelais and Montaigne. First, he was connected with the French "nouveau roman" with the special attention it paid to the quality of description. However, while the efforts of most authors of "nouveau roman" withered in a narrow narrative space, voluntarily chosen by them, and that space was overwhelmingly Western, Le Clézió differed, as he broke out of the "own," to reach the "other."

In the above-mentioned three stories the "other" is a child or a teenager with a pure soul, to whom the adults—those whose highest aspiration is to find their place by means of reason and force in the world of the "first"—cannot offer responses. "Lullaby did not think any more of school. It is so with the sea: it washes away earthy things, because it is more important than anything else. (---) the whole sea resembled a huge animal twisting its head and lashing the air with its tail. Lullaby felt very well. (---) She didn't think any more of streets, houses, cars or motorcycles."

Le Clézio has published about forty books. Volume should not be a determining factor in the spiritual field, but unfortunately it tends to be so. Few contemporary writers could have secured themselves a place in modern world literature by only one novel (of scarce two hundred pages) and a dozen stories, as was the case of the Mexican Juan Rulfo (whose *Pedro Páramo* has been translated into a great number of languages, Estonian included). Rulfo did not receive the Nobel Prize, but it hardly matters. Borges did not receive it either, nor Joyce nor Kafka.

What matters much more is the question about literature's message. Thus in comparison with Le Clézio or some other great contemporary writer, (post)modern Estonian authors of fictional prose notably cling to themselves. Attempts to reach out of oneself, to try to feel the "other," a different consciousness and culture, are extremely few. Yet it is an ancient wisdom that without feeling the "other," one cannot hope to know oneself.

Desert

Consider one of Le Clézio's most outstanding achievements, his novel *Désert* (1980; *Desert*). It was translated into Estonian in 1990, when Le Clézio probably could not even dream of one day receiving the Nobel Prize. It was a lucky intuition which led our Estonian translator Kristiina Ross to recognize early the value of the work. By contrast, the English translation of *Désert* (2009) was obviously triggered by Le Clézio's Nobel Prize, a much more commercial driving factor behind literature's intercultural reception.

In going to the "other," Le Clézio makes no compromises with the world of the "first." He is opposed to the attempts of the authors of "nouveau roman" to achieve special qualities by formal and linguistic games, and he also diverges from the sophisticated language employed by postmodern theoretical discourses. In *Desert* he writes simple phrases, but they are full of lyrical overtones. By such means he conveys the consciousness of the "other," whether a Moroccan adolescent girl or a poor dumb shepherd who cannot speak but who has been taught by desert silence and sea winds love's delicacy and tenderness, the feeling the poets of *dolce stil nuovo* tried to utter in the early Italian language, still in its virginal state.

By contrast, the West has developed its language in the Modern Era first and foremost in order to justify violating nature and indigenous people as if by a superiority of its language and reason or by a higher degree of its "own" civilization. The historical-epic background narrative in *Desert*, describing the cruel suppression of Morocco's independence, alludes ironically to that process. Le Clézio is a valiant writer who despite belonging himself to the "centre," revolts against it—in defense of "edges," in defense of nature and life.

Both in *Desert* and in the children's book there are symbols that should matter a lot to us here, on the "edge" of Europe. Do we really need to aspire at any cost to reach the "first" world? Is the worth of a nation not identical with its spirituality, creativity, and soul's quality, rather than with its earthly welfare? Would it not be better to try to create instead of a society based on the cult of reason and science (whose premonitions can be found in Jonathan Swift's *Gulliver's Travels* and Pierre Boule's *Planet of the Apes*) a harmony with nature around us, a solidarity with the "other"—so that it ceases to be the "other"—and to aspire to essential goodness that could also provide science with a new meaning?

LETTER 10

WHEN I BEGAN TO WRITE my series of letters to you, I did not plan in advance what topics I would treat. I only knew that I wanted to have at the core of my discussion the relationship between "self" and "other." In your *Essays*, despite their wide scope of topics, you certainly centre on the question of self-analysis, or how to understand oneself, and at the same time you include, more than any thinker before you, a dialogue with the "other," in its widest sense. It is quite clear also for me, that in trying to understand oneself, one cannot cope without watching the "other," or the world around us, while understanding the "other" cannot be detached from our "selves."

The way of cognition, greatly based on comparison, should be a ceaseless movement between "self" and "other." Final clarity or truth can never be achieved, but when we are in movement in ourselves, we certainly have the greatest chance to harmonize with the world, which at every moment, in every tiniest particle of time, changes. Maybe that movement in our selves, in harmony with the world's greater "self," could provide us some temporary satisfaction and happiness, until the dream of our lives in this world ends.

I am reluctant to speculate about the otherworld and things we really can never know or feel directly. No one has returned from there, to tell us first hand how it will be. We can only imagine it, as Dante Alighieri has done. I am too old to project any too optimistic future for humankind. In fact, as I write these lines to you, I am older than you were when you left this world. Is my life-experience richer than yours? Indeed I have been able to follow and take part in some of the most spectacular changes in the human communication. A century before your lifetime, book-printing brought about a revolution in the spread and the exchange of the human mind's products.

At the end of the 20th century, a similar revolution seems to have taken place with the introduction of internet communication and other miracles produced by electronic computing machines. These have tremendously accelerated all processes, good and bad. They have created an illusion of a rapid "leap" to a paradise on earth, but as soon as we move into the final stage of our individual lives, we realize that the illusion provided by technical progress offers us no comfort. It does not help us when we face the disappearance of our "self" from this world. Far more comfort comes from the love and understanding of others near us, or if we are left completely alone—also a part of human reality—we may still resort to faith that the spirit of the great totality, God, God-mother, or whatever we call the supreme Creator, does not abandon us completely and has compassion on us in our final earthly misery.

* * *

I know you, Montaigne, despised tyranny and ambition, the main cause of wars waged by men. However, because wars in your lifetime and in the past had been among the basic activities of men, you took them as natural and unavoidable. In your *Essays* you draw many examples from war experience, because in wars men were pushed to a crucial physical contact with death's breath, if not with death itself (because what death is we cannot know or feel, we can only perceive the air of its threshold).

Although you despised bookish knowledge, you were a very keen observer of such border or limit situations of our natural-physical existence, as described by numerous writers or warriors themselves in their work. In that sense, my life experience is much narrower than yours. I spent three years of my life in compulsory military service, but that was in peace-time. It was a light joke, an imitation of war activity, without ever entering a real battle.

To be honest, because I have lived in peace-time conditions, and had plenty of time to think about wars in the past, the greatest of which occurred during the scarce lapse of fifty years just immediately before I was born, it is hard for me to admit wars and military violence as something inevitable. Especially Erasmus, whose work I admire as much as yours, has made me realize that wars are among the greatest real follies of men. They contradict nature more than any other human activity. As my country, Estonia, has a tiny population of scarcely more than a million people, while the potential enemies are incomparably superior to us in their human, economic, and military resources, it seems to me ridiculous and grotesque that we at any cost try to imitate what is being done in other, bigger countries in this sense.

Instead, Estonia could provide Europe and the world a noble moral example by giving up its military forces. It could channel human and material resources wasted on its army to other, more constructive activities in society. The moral example given by such action to the world would be the best defense for the country. I know that many strong young men—and Estonia has quite a few such men—would willingly try their physical faculties in military actions, especially if they can gain some money. Such possibilities are not missing at all in the present-day world. Estonian young men are already active in bigger international military units in different parts of the world. I cannot see it as contradicting our nation's peaceful nature. Also, in Thomas More's *Utopia*, a peaceful island, mercenaries from the continent, especially from Switzerland, were employed as soldiers, whenever there was a need to defend Utopia against foreign invaders.

Naturally, I know very well it will not happen in Estonia in my lifetime. Males are overwhelmingly dominating the mechanism of political-economical power. There are plenty of myths (patriotism, national pride, etc.) from the past by which the society can easily be manipulated in favour of false male ideals, whatever the price a nation has to pay for them, in real terms. However, as for the whole world, some shifts of attitude and changes of climate in this field can be observed. Already at least one country with a population over a million people (Costa Rica, in Central America) has abolished its national armed forces. I have not been there myself, but as far as I know, Costa Rica, since giving up maintaining its army in 1949 has not been in any imminent danger of being invaded or annexed by any foreign country. Costa Rica is a symbol and an example of a peaceful way of national development in the American continent. The national resources relieved from maintaining an army have been used in Costa Rica for preserving its rich nature, as well as for other peaceful purposes.

Not long ago the majority of Latin American countries, quite on the contrary, were governed my military men or dictators. It is a highly significant change that today in nearly all Latin American countries military or autocratic rulers have been ousted from power and the countries have established democratic systems, whatever their difficulties and problems in this initial stage of transition. The role of women in this change has been exemplary from the very beginning. Even under dictatorships they have been the most active part of society in manifesting their sense for justice. Almost by a symbolic coincidence, some of the biggest South American countries, Brazil and Argentina, that in their history nearly always have been ruled my militaries or male dictators, in these days have or have had women as their democratically elected presidents.

Would monstrous wars, including both 20th century world wars, with their tens of millions of innocent victims, ever have been waged, had women's share in ruling the countries been greater? Even small cuts of military expenditure in the budget of the world superpowers would save millions of people dying daily from hunger around the world. What woman would approve it, if she is really free to speak out from her conscience? If women could rule the world—something that naturally would never happen—the world would not be without wars. However, rather than wars of senselessly killing masses of people, these would be wars of love. There, too, wounds and scars are deep, but still, they hardly contradict life on the earth but are part of it.

* * *

For a week here at the Rhodes' writers' creative house, internet connection was lost. Greek technicians could not find out where the problem was. Nobody seemed to be willing to take responsibility. My first reaction was to consider the incident ridiculously shameful. In my country, Estonia, which in our days is especially proud of its info-tech skills, a team of specialists would have solved such a problem without delay. Indeed, the Greek administrators, working in the writers' house, could not do their job, because almost everything in the present-day administrative field is dependent on computers and internet connection. We, writers or translators, still could work at our tasks of translating and writing, because the internet, though useful, is not in most cases an urgent primary need.

Working for a week without internet connection in the writers' house, I was reminded how easily a human being can be manipulated by the technical world and the big business related to it. We have unconsciously become part of it. However, when there is an interruption in this vortex in which we whirl, we understand that life can go on also without technical and business machinery. Without them, we may be able to meditate and write even more fruitfully, relying more on ourselves and expecting less from the exterior contour that surrounds us, with its illusionism ever blinding us.

I have lived for nearly a year in the U.S. without watching TV. Long before internet, at least since the 1950s and 60s, TV became the greatest visual seducing mechanism of humankind. Now, the same kind of seduction, based always on human weakness, exercising its power on one's sight and hearing, comes through the internet.

* * *

Males cannot be banished from the world. Women would never wish or seek it. Without the interaction of both genders, love, the great natural organ of perpetuating life, would be impossible for the majority of humans. I am not as sceptical about science as you, Montaigne. There are fields of science which beyond doubt have contributed to life. Besides, women have not been left aside at all. Thus in my day there are more women than men active as medical doctors in Estonia. You claim that nature itself should cure illnesses. It is true in part. We observe in animals that they, when ill, do not touch food, until they start to feel well again. Humans, unfortunately, have not been provided with such a subtle self-feeling of their state of health, as animals. They mostly still need specialized help from other people, more learned and experienced in medical knowledge than they themselves.

You lost most of your children at an early age, probably because medical care, provided by doctors in your day, was not sufficient. More than ten years ago I underwent a surgery. I believe without this intervention in the natural process of my illness I might have suffered from ever more serious health problems, if it had not come to worse. For you, life was a supreme value. And it is. It is possible you could have lived longer, at least to my age, and could have written even more fruitfully, had medical science been able to cure you of kidney stones, the cause of your death.

The question is not of banishing males, knowledge, or science from the world. It is rather of trying to find ways for restraining their alienated excesses. Women have demonstrated by the start of the 21st century that they are not at all intellectually or mentally weaker than men. They have become active in nearly all fields of human activity. In Western countries, most women work. They do not stay at home, as in the past. Women are also philosophers, even though until today, at least on the international scale, none of them has been able to rival the glories of creation of their male colleagues.

Yet I do not think women should become such a subject than would constitute another, complementary "self," equal in its qualities to the "self" established by males. It would be an absolute nonsense if male "self," doubled in its energy by womankind's "self," would ever more rapidly rush along the path of "progress," which until now has mainly meant destruction of nature and humiliation of the "other," in the broadest sense.

Recent Western history has shown that women, though talented also in science and business, still tend to avoid taking big risks, preferring instead to control what they do, take full responsibility for what they feel. Thus one may be sure that nearly all the CEOs of international corporations in science, industry, and business, that is, mechanisms moving the material processes of the human world, are males. Thanks to big risks they take, a great number of them have become incredibly rich. Politicians, who have been elected by people to restrain these excesses, become themselves involved in big dirty business. From time to time they are caught at their corrupt dealings, brought to justice and sometimes even—when their friends, astute lawyers, fail to invent excuses—put into prison. One may be sure that in most cases these mega-criminals are males.

Women have by far a deeper sense for justice. They can be sharper than men in intimate love affairs, even astute. However, with the exception of the occasional "Lady Macbeth" and some "iron ladies"—in any case a tiny minority of women, when it comes to the interests of the "other" and the matters of an entire society, women generally avoid embracing an anonymity that escapes their senses. They feel more deeply, they are more sensible, and therefore take more responsibility for their actions than men.

For that reason I am quite convinced that if women's role in different spheres of social action increases, new hopes to improve the situation on the earth of the "other," the "second" or the "third" or whatever we call all living nature not conforming with the predominant thinking and way of being of Western-formed males, may emerge in the long run. Science long ago proved that in human beings one of the cerebral hemispheres governs our reason's choices, while the other hemisphere feeds our feelings and emotions. This is so both in men and women.

Yuri Lotman was fascinated by the interaction of our brain hemispheres. Gradually he came to imagine a totality that he called "semiosphere." There, according to his ideas, an ideal ground is formed for a fruitful dialogue between the huge biosphere and the brain-work of the humans, the noo-sphere. In the same intersection area, "explosions" could take place, leading to new quality in culture, as well as influencing all human existence. Once we accept the fruitful interaction of our both cerebral hemispheres, why not accept men and women as equal, though different, natural "selves"?

Besides, as the cultural "explosion" on the transition period from the late Middle Ages to the Renaissance has wonderfully proved in the example of culture and life in general, the presence of women and their beauty can definitely free males from their coarseness and primitive egoism, as well as improve their human qualities. It does not mean at all that males would not be males any more. They will be males as they always have been, but they could become wiser, more open to the senses, beauty, and the "other."

You, Montaigne, liked women. I, too, like them. I believe together we, a minority of men of the land of the dead as well the living—philosophers, poets, whatever men, why not men of science?—have been called to this world to support women in their arduous action in asserting their "self" more completely than in the past, eliminating reduction by males to the humble function of man's serf and his "rib."

Like you, I am sceptical by nature. I do not really believe any quick changes possible. I even do not have much faith in Lotmanian "leaps," if we understand by them changes taking place in short decades. Substantial changes can never ignore spiritual aspects. Yet relying on the evidence of the course of history so far, I am convinced that a gradual modification in the interrelation between human genders and their "selves" can lead in the future not only philosophy, but also science, to admit a conclusion that was absolutely natural for you, Montaigne: whatever our faults and stumbling, during the brief second of life (or, of the dream of life) given to us, there can hardly be a truer aim of our action on the earth than virtue.

* * *

For a socio-cultural renovation of today's world, acrobatics and masochism of the body (economy) and the mind (logo-centrism) scarcely suffice. Their effect will always remain on the surface of being, without penetrating its interiority. They are pleasures and joys of a tiny minority or a generic-sexual sect. A deeper renovation should embrace and penetrate our spiritual and ethical being. It is not really important what name we give it at a determined moment in history: 'trans-modernism' or something different. Once a change capable of proving its reality has taken place, it will receive its name or perhaps have several names at once.

Such a change can only be a slow movement that recuperates spiritual and creative values of the past. It is not only eco-logical, but at the same time, eco-sensible. In other words, it needs not only to know the order of our common *oikos,* but, simultaneously, to feel, perceive, intuit the big house that we share with others. It means a symbiotic process, with all our creative faculties—mind, feelings, intellect and passion—participating, intertwined and not separated, both in man and woman, in the search of a new equilibrium with nature of which we are part.

Index of Names

Alas, Arvo
Albee, Edward
Aleixandre, Vicente
Aristotle
Avellaneda, Alonso Fernández de
Azorín

Bakhtin, Mikhail
Balzac, Honoré de
Barnet, Miguel
Baroja, Pío
Beecher Stowe, Harriet
Blake, William
Boccaccio, Giovanni
Borges, Jorge Luis
Boulle, Pierre
Brontë, Charlotte
Brontë, Emily
Byron, George Gordon

Caballero, Fernán (Cecilia Böhl de Faber)
Calderón de la Barca, Pedro
Capote, Truman
Castro, Fidel
Castro, Rosalía de

Cervantes, Miguel de
Charlemagne
Chaucer, Geoffrey
Coleridge, Samuel Taylor
Cooper, James Fenimore
Cruz, Juana Inés de la

Dalí, Salvador
Dante Alighieri
Danton, Georges Jacques
Defoe, Daniel
Derrida, Jacques
Descartes, René
Dickens, Charles
Dickinson, Emily
Diderot, Denis
Donne, John
Dostoyevsky, Fyodor
Du Bellay, Joachim

Eliot, George (Mary Ann Evans)
Eliot, T(homas) S(tearns)
Erasmus, Desiderius

Faulkner, William
Fernández de Oviedo, Gonzalo
Flaubert, Gustave
Forster, E(Edward). M(organ).
Foucault, Michel

García Lorca, Federico
García Márquez, Gabriel
Goethe, Johann Wolfgang (von)
Gómez de Avellaneda, Gertrudis

Góngora, Luis de
Gorbachev, Mikhail
Gracián, Baltasar

Hegel, Georg Wilhelm Friedrich
Heine, Heinrich
Henry VIII
Herder, Johann Gottfried
Hitler, Adolf
Hix, H(arvey) L(ee)
Horn, W. O. von
Høeg, Peter
Hugo, Victor
Huxley, Aldous

Ibarbourou, Juana de
Ibsen, Henrik

Jiménez, Juan Ramón
Joyce, James

Kaalep, Ain
Kafka, Franz
Koidula, Lydia
Kreutzwald, Friedrich Reinhold
Kross, Jaan

Labé, Louise
La Fayette (*Marie-Madeleine* Pioche de La Vergne)
Lagerlöf, Selma
Las Casas, Bartolomé de
Lawrence, David Herbert
Le Clézio, Jean Marie Gustave
Lias, Ruth

Liiv, Juhan
Lotman, Yuri M.
Lowell, Amy

Machado, Antonio
Macpherson, James
Mao Zedong
Marguerite de Navarre
Marie de France
Marino, Giambattista
Marlowe, Chistopher
Marx, Karl
Matto de Turner, Clorinda
Mérimée, Prosper
Merkel, Angela
Michelson, Helle
Mistral, Gabriela
Molière (Jean Baptiste Poquelin)
More, Thomas
Mussolini, Benito

Neruda, Pablo
Nietzsche, Friedrich
Nobel, Alfred

Obama, Barack
Ojamaa, Ott
Oras, Ants
Ortega y Gasset, José

Pascal, Blaise
Petrarch, Francesco
Plato
Plutarch
Poe, Edgar Allan

Pound, Ezra
Proust, Marcel
Pulci, Luigi

Quevedo, Francisco de

Rabelais, François
Rand, Esta
Robespierre, Maximilien de
Rojas, Fernando de
Ronsard, Pierre de
Ross, Kristiina
Rousseau, Jean-Jacques
Rulfo, Juan
Rummo, Linda

Saagpakk, Paul F.
Sakharov, Andrei
Saint-Just, Louis Antoine de
Sand, George (Lucile Aurore Dupin Dudevant)
Sang, August
Sartre, Jean-Paul
Saussure, Ferdinand de
Schiller, Friedrich
Scott, Walter
Screech, M. A.
Sebond, Raymond
Selkirk, Alexander
Semper, Johannes
Shakespeare, William
Shapiro, Adolf
Shelley, Percy Bysshe
Sivers, Fanny de
Sokrates
Soomere, Krista

Södergran, Edith
Stalin, Iosif
Stendhal
Sterne, Laurence
Swift, Jonathan

Tammsaare, Anton Hansen
Tirso de Molina (Gabriel Téllez)
Torpats, Ülo
Trummal, Albert
Tuglas, Friedebert

Unamuno, Miguel de
Under, Marie
Undset, Sigrid
Unt, Mati

Üksküla, Aarne

Vega, Félix Lope de
Vergilius
Verne, Jules
Vidal, Gore
Voltaire

Whitman, Walt
Wilde, Oscar
Woolf, Virginia

Yeltsin, Boris

Zeno
Zola, Émile

About the Author

Jüri Talvet (born in 1945 in Pärnu, Estonia) received his PhD degree in Western literatures from Leningrad University (1981). Since 1992 he has Chaired World Literature at the University of Tartu, where he also founded Spanish Studies and *Interlitteraria*. His personal poetic anthology *Eesti eleegia ja teisi luuletusi 1981–2012* (Estonian Elegy and Other Poems Tartu, 2014, 375 pp) gathers more than 400 poems. His poetry and essays have been translated into a number of languages. In English, Guernica has previously published *A Call for Cultural Symbiosis* (2005), *Estonian Elegy* (2008), *Of Snow, of Soul* (2010). *Yet, Love, Illumine Us* appeared in 2018 in the US (Červena Barvá Press). Talvet has been awarded the Juhan Smuul Annual Prize of Literature (1986), Juhan Liiv Poetry Prize (1997), Ivar Ivask Memorial Prize of Essay and Poetry (2002) and other distinctions. Since 2016 he is an ordinary member of Academia Europaea.

About the Translator

H. L. Hix received his PhD in Philosophy from the University of Texas. He has taught at Kansas City Art Institute, held an administrative post at Cleveland Institute of Art, been a visiting professor at Shanghai University, and been Fulbright Distinguished Chair at Yonsei University in Seoul. Currently he holds a joint appointment in philosophy and creative writing at the University of Wyoming. His prior collaborations with Jüri Talvet include an edition of the poems of Juhan Liiv, *Snow Drifts, I Sing*, published by Guernica in 2013. His own recent books include a poetry collection, *Rain Inscription* (Etruscan Press, 2017), an essay collection, *Demonstrategy* (Etruscan, 2019), and an art/poetry anthology, *Ley Lines* (Wilfrid Laurier Univ. Press, 2014). His poetry collection *Chromatic* was a 2006 finalist for the National Book Award.